Knowledge Centric Management

Urgent recommendations and a practical and pragmatic framework to become a knowledge centric organisation.

Knowledge Centric Management

First published in 2011 by Ecademy Press

48 St Vincent Drive, St Albans, Hertfordshire, AL1 5SJ

info@ecademy-press.com www.ecademy-press.com

Printed and Bound by Lightning Source in the UK and USA

Set by Duncan McKean

Printed on acid-free paper from managed forests.

This book is printed on demand, so no copies will be remaindered or pulped.

ISBN 978-1-907722-26-4

The right of Hans van Heghe to be identified as the author of this work has been asserted in accordance with sections 77 and 78 of the Copyright Designs and Patents Act 1988.

A CIP catalogue record for this book is available from the British Library.

All rights reserved. No part of this work may be reproduced in any material form (including photocopying or storing in any medium by electronic means and whether or not transiently or incidentally to some other use of this publication) without the written permission of the copyright holder except in accordance with the provisions of the Copyright, Designs and Patents Act 1988. Applications for the Copyright holders' written permission to reproduce any part of this publication should be addressed to the publishers.

The purpose of this book is to educate and entertain. The author and Ecademy Press shall have neither liability nor responsibility to any person or entity with respect to any loss or damage caused, or alleged to have been caused, directly or indirectly, by the information contained in this book. If you do not wish to be bound by the above, you may return this book to the place where you purchased it or to the publisher for a full refund.

Copyright © 2011

Hans van Heghe

Knowledge Centric Management

Preface

The rules were simple. Raise your arm and finger, stay seated, do not shout. We all knew what was expected of us. But when a lot of competitors were fighting for attention, we all pushed the admissible to the limit – and a little further. Left and right and behind, someone would gradually disconnect from a chair and suppressed noises would rise from closed mouths. Every brain emitted one, and only one, strong message: "Me! Me! Choose me!"

Eventually the teacher would look at one of us and the chosen pupil was allowed to provide the answer to the question that was asked seconds before by the almighty teaching professional. Sometimes we got lucky and the poor devil that was chosen provided the wrong answer. Within a split-second, arms shot up into the air, bottoms were lifted and less suppressed noises filled the classroom. "Me! Me! Choose me."

I guess all of us remember those days. We were 10 years young and knowing the right answer was what school life was all about. Correct answers raised the appreciation the teacher had for us. At the same time it triggered envy from classmates. Those who scored too well did so at the risk of becoming social outcasts.

I refer to that period in life as the *'I know'* era, filled with youngsters who desperately wanted to be an 'I Know Person'. Actually I should call it the *'I know what the teacher wants me to know'* period. Whether the knowledge was relevant to my further development was ... well ... irrelevant. Pleasing the teacher was the mission.

Life went on and school became tougher. Soon it became impossible to know everything the multiple teachers wanted me to know. That led to a period I call the *'What should I know?'* phase. Too much knowledge was available and it became important to select only what I really needed – hoping that this would fit into my limited memory capacity. The selection criteria were simple: I needed to know what was going to be asked during the exams. We all became 'What Should I Know People'.

When school was over, work life started. The small number of teachers that used to guide me was replaced by hundreds, thousands of colleagues, all of whom carried pieces of wisdom and knowledge. I was soon to find out that fellow employees were sources of information that needed to be considered carefully. Often the quality of the guidance was very good, but even more often the information was incomplete, incorrect or even misleading. The *'Who really knows?'* period had started. My search for information had become a quest to find the people who really knew.

Today you decided to start reading Hans Van Heghe's new book on Knowledge Management. A wise decision. Your timing is perfect. We live in a knowledge economy where intellectual property and experience have monetary values that often stretch beyond imagination. Disaster is, however, about to strike Western Europe. Age demographics are rapidly closing in on us. Over the coming seven years a massive number of highly-skilled professionals will retire. With them decades of experience will vanish from the intellectual capital of our companies. To add to the problem, the same age demographics dictate a far smaller inflow of skills and knowledge. The number of people retiring is significantly higher than the number of students exchanging school life for paid jobs.

Companies invest massively to protect their intellectual property. Bullet-proof legislation is demanded. Information systems are shielded. Research labs are guarded by specialised firms. The knowledge and experience drain resulting from the dreaded age demographics monster is, however, far more dangerous than industrial espionage. It is not like a sudden disease one catches and that doctors treat immediately. It is a camouflaged killer that slowly destroys you. By the time it lays off its camouflage, the damage is likely to be irreversible.

But not for you.

You bought Hans' book, so you are interested in Knowledge Management. KM indeed holds one of the keys to fight brain drain successfully. When applied intelligently it enables you to capture the existing knowledge about your processes, your business models, your information systems, your company, your success. Stored information, however, is only valuable if the pieces of information one needs can be retrieved easily by the people who need them – or even better, if they are presented to the folks who are likely to need them, but who may not even know they exist. That is where Knowledge Management starts to produce a return on investment.

At the beginning of my career I was a teacher. I loved passing on knowledge, building skills, sculpturing attitudes, helping youngsters to get ready for shaping their own lives. Good teachers have the ability to explain complex matters in easy to understand language. Firms now need to become teachers, writing the knowledge book of their own companies and then passing on the information to new employees, helping them to acquire skills and building experience at a faster pace than has ever happened in the past.

This book will help you in your quest for knowledge preservation and creation. Use the 'I Know People'. They will willingly provide you with tons of information. They have the knowledge and are eager to share it. Many of them already do so on all kinds of social media. Have the 'What Should I Know People' help you prioritise your tasks, but remember that what seems anecdotal today may be of value tomorrow. Use the *'Who Really Knows?'* experience extensively to find the correct information – as often what you find will be only part of the truth, or simply wrong.

Good luck. And… hurry, the clock is ticking.

Marc Lambotte
Vice President and General Manager, Unisys, Benelux & Nordics

Contents

Preface	i
Introduction	vii
Part 1	1
A few thoughts on knowledge management	1
The story of Alex and Benjamin	3
Challenges or problems?	4
The tipping point	6
Solutions can be that simple!	7
And now for the challenges	10
Personal experiences and reflections	11
Is there really a need for Knowledge Management?	13
From an operational economy towards a knowledge-driven economy	14
Data, information, knowledge	15
Your information and expertise count	20
Knowledge is not new	21
Information overload	25
Knowledge issues	26
What international studies say	28
Opportunities for improvement	32
Quotes from leading people	33
Knowledge from a management perspective	35
Personal experiences and reflections	36
My lessons learned	37
On information and knowledge	38
On people and change	42
On Knowledge Management itself	45
Personal experiences and reflections	50

PART II	53
A Knowledge Management framework	53
Knowledge Management framework	55
A world of Knowledge	56
Knowledge about Knowledge Management	57
The Knowledge Management building blocks	59
Knowledge worker perspective	61
Knowledge organisation perspective	62
Overview	63
Personal experiences and reflections	64
Knowledge about Knowledge Management	65
Human competences	66
Knowledge sources	67
Knowledge logistics	68
Parameters for success	75
Personal experiences and reflections	79
The Knowledge Management building blocks	81
Knowledge value	82
JERI – Just Enough Relevant Information, when and where needed	
	84
Context and model	85
Subjective profiles	90
Business processes	91
Communication and writing	94
Communities	101
Knowledge Management and learning	102
Securing versus securing	103
Personal experiences and reflections	104
Knowledge worker perspective	105
Too much information	106
Not enough knowledge	109
Lost knowledge	111
Personal experiences and reflections	114

Knowledge organisation perspective   *115*
   Operational   *116*
   Tactical   *119*
   Strategic   *122*
   Personal experiences and reflections   *127*

PART III — 129
Results of growing Knowledge centric management — 129

Goal and objective of Knowledge Management — 131
Becoming knowledge-driven — 132
Knowledge centric management — 133
Promote re-use! — 134
Personal experiences and reflections — 135

Growing versus Maturity — 137
Evolution as a knowledge organisation — 138
Growth process — 143
Personal experiences and reflections — 145

Roll-out of Knowledge Management — 147
Preparatory steps — 148
A growing process — 150
Personal experiences and reflections — 156

Measuring your evolution — 157
After the implementation — 158
24 elements to evaluate Knowledge Management, today and tomorrow — 159
Personal experiences and reflections — 165

The value of Knowledge Management — 167
Value elements — 168
For the knowledge worker — 169
For the knowledge organisation — 170
Measuring value of Knowledge Management — 171
Personal experiences and reflections — 176

Knowledge Management from a macro-economic perspective — 179
External Knowledge Management — 180
From a government perspective — 181
From a sector perspective — 183
Personal experiences and reflections — 185

PART IV	187
A new approach: Knowledge Management made easy and quick	187
A new approach	189
Classic Knowledge Management approaches	190
Question-driven approach	192
What is a question-driven solution?	193
Essential features	196
Personal experiences and reflections	197
Implementing Knowledge Management easily with quick wins	199
Overview	200
Preparation phase	201
Dynamic operational phase	204
Extension phase	206
Personal experiences and reflections	208
Results and reports	209
Results	210
Reports	215
Personal experiences and reflections	216
Appendices	219
Author	221
ICMS Group	223
TiNK method	225

Introduction

This book has multiple objectives for different kinds of presidents, directors and managers in an organisation.

Many organisations are implementing *ERP, CRM* and other expensive acronyms. Here and there, the term *Knowledge Management* is mentioned.

It is becoming more and more clear: we live and work in a *knowledge economy*. Your knowledge and expertise – together with quality and service level – is what makes your organisation different from your competition or new players in your market.

BUT HOW DO YOU START?

My four main objectives of this book – after all these years of intellectual challenges on Knowledge Management – are:

- ▷ Provide you with knowledge on Knowledge Management
  helping you to better understand the complete picture
  instead of just fragments

- ▷ Tell you about my lessons learned
  sharing the do's and the don'ts with you
  allowing you to re-use and get value out of these experiences
- ▷ Provide you with a pragmatic and usable framework
  helping your organisation to start with Knowledge Management
  and grow towards a knowledge centric organisation
- ▷ Explain a new innovative and pragmatic approach (and technology)
  to set up Knowledge Management fast and easily
  delivering immediately direct results (for the user)
  and indirect results (for the management)

Each of these objectives corresponds to a main part of this book.

These main parts can be read independently from each other and in a different order.

This book will provide you with the fundamentals and the required know-how to start implementing Knowledge Management in your organisation.

It is my belief and conviction that Knowledge Management is not an independent objective. Knowledge Management is an instrument to turn your organisation into a knowledge centric organisation, an organisation where management acts based on available knowledge.

'Knowledge Centric Management' is, in this regard, a logical and down-to-earth title describing the main objective we are all facing in this Knowledge Economy.

At the end of each chapter you will find some valid exercises and a link towards *www.knowliah.eu/kcm*

This site contains a knowledge base with interaction and discussion capabilities also containing extra exercises, cases and solutions to the exercises.

Enjoy...

Hans Van Heghe
President and Founder of ICMS Group

Part I

A FEW THOUGHTS ON KNOWLEDGE MANAGEMENT

This section discusses my personal lessons learned.

After 12 years of practising Knowledge Management in hundreds of organisations across different sectors, big and small, it is time for a wrap-up.

As such, this section contains:

- ▷ A story about the positive impact of Knowledge Management in an organisation
- ▷ Reflections and confirmations
  with regard to the need for Knowledge Management in any type of organisation
- ▷ My personal lessons learned
  what really matters and
  what is accessory in this domain

The story of Alex and Benjamin

How Alex and Benjamin became good friends.

It might also happen to you...
Are you Benjamin or Alex?

CHALLENGES OR PROBLEMS?

Benjamin, who very recently turned 40, celebrates his fifth year with SmartCorp today. He is the Chief Operations Officer of SmartCorp, a medium-sized, well respected knowledge economy organisation. Benjamin is looking forward to the noon luncheon his Chief Executive Officer, Boris, will invite him to at his preferred Italian eatery. It's a bright and sunny day, and while work on occasions has been challenging, days like these, being celebrated by colleagues, make up for all those nights of hard labour. He enters his office at the SmartCorp building, whistling the latest of the greatest hits he listened to on his radio. It's going to be a great day... Or is it?

Benjamin is quickly led to questioning his slightly presumptive and quite erroneous assessment of the day when he sees **Christopher** positioned at the edge of his desk. Christopher looks far from happy, and launches into a complex and convoluted story about his collaborator Denis, who sent the wrong version of a specifications document to one of their key clients. Said client was on the phone to Christopher about 10 minutes after receipt of the document, complaining about lack of professionalism, lack of quality, non-covered risks for themselves as well as for SmartCorp.

After some poking around, Christopher finds out that he had not been informed of the promises made by **Eric**, the account manager, to this client. Their promises turn out to be almost impossible to fulfil and aren't even within the scope of services of SmartCorp.

Big issue. Christopher, being on a roll, continues fulminating about a problem with another important client, which had been timely flagged by the client but sat in the mailbox of **Frank**, a collaborator on extended leave. With an "And the root cause of this is your ICT department!" Christopher storms out, leaving a flabbergasted Benjamin gasping for air. And he hasn't even made it to his chair yet.

Barely avoiding being pinned behind his own door trying to hang up his jacket, Benjamin is seized by **Gabrielle**, the head of the server room. She tells him about big issues with the servers which kept her staff in until the early hours. The 500 gigabyte additional server space installed only five months ago has filled up, with all servers running in excess of 95% capacity, resulting in significant quality of service problems at the user end. The memories of the bright and shiny faces of his kids wishing him a wonderful day at the office have all but disappeared, leaving large dark thunderclouds stacking up at his mental horizon. It looks like more than rain – it looks like a full hurricane warning needs to come into effect, now.

And not a moment too soon. The office hurricane, **Helen**, formally known as SmartCorp's legal counsel, seizes control of his office barely seconds after Gabrielle has left it. She had to revise multiple contracts, each written by another of SmartCorp's account managers, each with different varieties of the general terms and conditions, none of them complete, and quite a number of them exposing SmartCorp to significant risks which could have been avoided if they had listened to her and used the standards available on the shared drive. Benjamin recovers remarkably under the onslaught, and has the presence of mind to call in a few of the account managers that happen to be in the office. They claim they cannot begin to understand the shared drive folder structure Helen has set up. Benjamin tactically directs the hostilities to take place outside his door, to allow him to think over what happened in the past minutes, and the warring parties leave.

Leaning back, he takes a deep breath and a sip of coffee, only to be interrupted by the insistent 'bling' of his Blackberry. He chokes, spilling coffee all over his shirt, and swears several profanities before looking at the screen of his PDA. It is **Isabel**, the R&D manager, with an urgent request for the identification of a specialist in risk management for one of their prime research projects.

Benjamin does the only thing he can do at this point. He runs... Yet another day from hell and it is only **8.23**. He likes challenges but he'd rather be working on strategic ideas than putting out fires all the time. The sun is shining brightly, and he already regrets not having taken the day off to tour the coastline in his new convertible.

THE TIPPING POINT

With hindsight, although **Benjamin** does not realize it, **8:27:29** becomes the tipping point of the day. This is the moment when Benjamin encounters Alex at the water cooler. **Alex** is the innovation manager of SmartCorp, always looking for ideal solutions and methodologies to optimise the internal processes of the organisation. A relative stranger to Alex, Benjamin feels strangely inclined to share the horror story of the morning with him.

Alex, a kind and bright-eyed 30-something, listens emphatically and smiles as the story twists and turns to Benjamin's leap for freedom for the water cooler. He appears to find the entire story highly entertaining. Having arrived at the end, Benjamin realises the conversation has been pretty one-sided and enquires politely as to the state of Alex's initiatives.

Still smiling, **Alex** starts talking about the essential nature of information, communication and knowledge in an organisation. He explains how SmartCorp has a lot of smart people, doing smart things, but they appear to miss significant opportunities to use these smarts in a constructive, value-added manner. Benjamin starts to realise that these are exactly the issues he has been confronted with this morning. "You probably have no solution for these issues, have you?" he implores.

Alex just smiles, and beckons Benjamin to follow him to his office. **Benjamin** starts to get an inkling of an idea that this young innovation manager might have a solution for at least some of his issues, and better understands that Cheshire cat smile. And he plunges down the rabbit hole.

SOLUTIONS CAN BE THAT SIMPLE!

Benjamin and Alex join **Jacob**, one of the innovation team managers. "Jacob, can you please show TiNK®4U to Benjamin?" Alex addresses Jacob, and leaning over to Benjamin, he says, "We'll start with the server issue of Gabrielle." Alex explains the new ICMS Group technology which SmartCorp is testing.

Gabrielle's garbage

Jacob slides behind his computer, logs in to TiNK®4U and clicks a couple of buttons in the **Administrator** interface. Instantaneously, a report with groups of files and a couple of figures appears. Jacob quickly reviews the data, and explains to Benjamin: "31.24% of the 2.5 terabytes of disk space on the server appears to be filled with redundant files and different versions of files already present elsewhere on the network. The report you see on the screen details the exact files which are responsible for these redundancies. We can use the information contained in the report to launch the clean-up operation, either manually or fully automatic, and reduce the versioning to the bare minimum."

Alex briefly flashes the famous Alice in Wonderland cat's smile. "One problem resolved, as well as a solution to keep this issue under control in the future," he states categorically. "On to the next issue."

Helen's hiccup

Tapping into the TiNK®4U interface, Jacob accesses the **BROWSE** functionality. He orders the system to create a virtual folder structure according to type of information – standard components. The system immediately shows a tree structure with all types of information, among which is legal information. He selects legal information and the system replies with a sub-branch within which 'standard components – contracts' is displayed. Selecting this, the system displays a list of all legal contract components with the indication of whether they are mandatory or optional. Jacob then shows Benjamin how to get the same crucial information from a number of different possible angles.

"I do believe this addresses our legal counsel's key issue, both for now and for the future, does it not?" Alex asks Benjamin with a mock grin. Benjamin can only nod, but a hint of a smile starts to show on his face. He asks Alex whether it would be possible to build a solution which would create a contract with the correct legal clauses based on a few simple rules. Alex smiles: "We're one step ahead of you there, dear Benjamin, we're currently implementing TiNK®cdg, another ICMS Group solution, which will allow us to do just that."

Eric's entanglement

"But why don't you take the wheel of my shiny new car?" Alex invites Benjamin to sit down and assume the controls of TiNK®4U. At first a little hesitant, Benjamin quickly warms to the **no-nonsense** interface. He creates a virtual folder according to client/project/subproject and immediately identifies the different versions of the document Eric had been working on, both in the document management system and on the file servers. Backing up, he tries to create a different virtual folder according to status/information type/author and again finds all the documents.

"This is amazing," he shouts. "Anyone can browse the available information from their own specific context... why didn't we buy this sooner?"

"I know," Alex replies, "but you still have a few open issues, haven't you?" Again the Cheshire cat smile flashes across his face, as he takes Benjamin's Blackberry out of his hands and scrolls quickly to Isabel's urgent message.

Isabel's issue

Jacob takes control of the chair and keyboard, and Alex asks him to enter a couple of keywords on the expertise requirements regarding risk management which Isabel is looking for, reading them off Benjamin's Blackberry. Jacob enters the information in the **EXPERTISE** functionality and a list of collaborators flashes on screen, with a percentage of relevance regarding experience and speciality in the matter. Much to his surprise, Benjamin finds that the person he was planning on recommending to Isabel only ranks fifth, with three times less relevant experience than the top two selected by the system. Confessing this to Alex, the innovation manager simply shrugs and says he had the same thing happen to him a couple of times in the past few days. The TiNK®4U tool has proven to be an eye-opener, even for people with many years of experience in the company. "We really don't know what we know, but we are starting to know we don't know."

With four out of six problems solved, Benjamin starts thinking about his lunch again.

Christopher's calamity

Benjamin dictates a couple of terms which characterise the **required knowledge** concerning the solutions as promised by Eric the account manager to the critical client. After two seconds, the system comes back with information which shows that, two months ago, a prototype solving that specific problem was built by the R&D department. The system also indicates the two specialists that had been working on the prototype. Alex explains the way in which TiNK®4U identifies knowledge **traces** based on information and communication from experts, as profiled in the system. "Guess what, we might finally be done with reinventing the wheel!" Alex exclaims.

Frank's folly

Alex sits down behind the keyboard and starts querying the system for Frank's emails. In a few seconds, he not only finds all these mails but also every mail sent pertaining to the subject. It becomes crystal clear that Christopher had been copied in with of most of the critical mails, and that he was more than capable of handling the problem himself before it spun out of **control**. Alex configures a simple security rule which allows Christopher to query all emails on his projects with this particular client. "There we go," Alex states, "no more hiding behind miscommunication. Each of us can be informed, and will have just enough relevant information available at all times to provide due diligence to our clients, and ultimately our shareholders. And that, dear Benjamin, is, I believe, six for six!"

AND NOW FOR THE CHALLENGES

At last, Benjamin will have **adequate time** to address the key business challenges, those challenges which will generate additional **revenue** and higher **margins**. He feels happy again, and knows what he will be talking about to his CEO.

And Alex, well, he felt **extremely happy** about a job well done. He realised ICMS Group was a **key partner** and supplier, with a clear vision and operational approach. "Mmm, it took 10 minutes to address Benjamin's problems... I wonder which quantum improvements we'll see when we roll out this solution to our entire organisation... the only issue Benjamin will have is to find the car keys to his sweet convertible."

And whistling softly while spinning the key of the blue Boxster on his finger, he walked off to the parking lot, to go and collect his wife for the promised day at the beach. After all, he had only come into work to bring back the keys to the stick shift he blew up the day before.

PERSONAL EXPERIENCES AND REFLECTIONS

What were your personal experiences on knowledge bottlenecks?

What are the most important ones in your organisation?

How would you approach those challenges?

- ▷ More hardware?
- ▷ Outsourcing?
- ▷ Throw away documents and emails?
- ▷ Drop it in the cloud?
- ▷ Hire more people?
- ▷ Let it be?
- ▷ Etc.

Have a look on www.knowliah.eu/kcm/1 for other questions, ideas, discussion and answers on this topic.

Is there really a need for Knowledge Management?

From an operational economy towards a knowledge-driven economy

Even though the financial crisis and global warming make it less visible, our economy really is changing from an operational economy to a knowledge-driven economy.

For western organisations especially, the production of goods or the delivery of services is no longer of paramount importance. That place has been taken by the development, management and deployment of new knowledge. The organisations of the future are those organisations that are able to valorise their knowledge in the quickest and most efficient way.

Thirty years ago, a customer was happy with a product as such. After that, a product with accompanying services became the credo. Today, customers not only want a product with accompanying services, but they also want to be supplied with the necessary knowledge and expertise for using the product in an optimal way.

Numbers are not what is most important here (despite the yearly increase by +/- 10%), that would be the information and validated knowledge of an organisation. Information and knowledge volumes that almost double every year.

Data, information, knowledge

Overview

Every day, we use a number of terms without giving a moment's thought, or paying enough attention, to the difference between these terms. The concepts of *data, information* and *knowledge* are no exception to this rule.

At the top of the pyramid describing the content of the human mind, there is **wisdom**. At the level below, there is **understanding**, followed by **knowledge, information** and **data**. Each category includes the underlying category: wisdom cannot exist without understanding, and understanding relies on knowledge. The human mind consists of roughly 40% data, supplemented with 30% information, 20% knowledge, 10% understanding and hardly any wisdom.

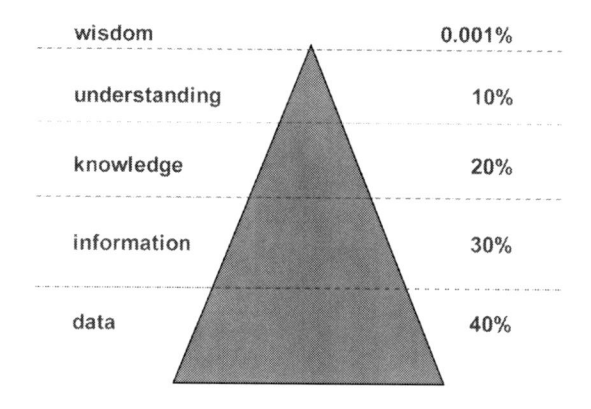

```
wisdom              0.001%
understanding       10%
knowledge           20%
information         30%
data                40%
```

Alzo sprach Russell L. Ackoff in 'From data to Wisdom' (Informatie, 1990)

In our daily language, data and information are often used as synonyms, but there really is a difference between the two. To put it simplistically, data is the raw material ('meaning*less* information') and information is the finished product ('meaning*ful* data'). Data is a product of observation; information is a product of interpretation.

Data = meaningless information

Data can be best described as 'meaningless information'. Data is:

- ▷ Groups of randomly-used symbols that represent properties ('attributes') of objects ('things'), events ('actions') and their surroundings; they are the product of observation
- ▷ An (objective) representation of facts, concepts, instructions or ideas in a formalised way, thereby facilitating communication, interpretation or manipulation by means of a process

Data can consist of letters, numbers and/or symbols with a special meaning (e.g. +, % and *).

Data consists of individual pieces of information, as can be found in regular files (flat files), hierarchical files (databases), etc. The relationship between these pieces of information is not defined, nor can it be derived intuitively. As mentioned previously, we are dealing with a random representation of facts and observations, and this is not really relevant.

Data as such is not that valuable. When we link facts and data to information about the relationships between them, then we have knowledge. Knowledge is more valuable than information.

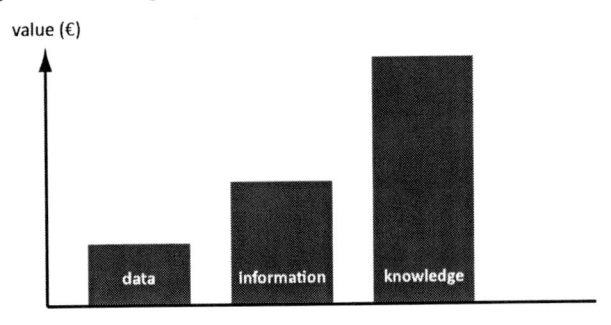

Relative value of data

BI – Business Intelligence – helps us to transform data into information.

Information = meaningful data

If we refer to data as 'meaningless information', then we can also refer to information as 'meaningful data'.

So, information is the meaning a person expresses through or derives from data.

The distinction between data and information is functional, not structural; data has no value as long as it has not been processed into a usable (i.e. relevant to the receiver) form.

Only when people do something with data, process it to add value to it, is information created. The fact (i.e. data) that there is a naked woman walking next to me is, in itself, no cause for the police to turn out. The situation changes, however, if I add the piece of data that I am in the middle of Trafalgar Square in London.

An organisation will want to have as much information as possible and as little data as possible.

Information in its true sense concerns data that has been grouped together to demonstrate certain associations. The relationship is obvious, but only thanks to the logical grouping, and the relationship is context-dependent. Information is more valuable than mere data.

Indeed, information consists of data that has been linked together and interpreted. This is also why different people may come to completely different insights, and thus decisions, on the basis of the same data (information). Interpretation is a special kind of processing that is only reserved for humans; it requires associative ability, which is something that computers and other machines lack completely.

The receiver has the final say: the receiver — not the sender — of a message decides whether or not something is information.

Information can be divided into *notifying* information, *explanatory* information and *directing* information. After something has been notified, an explanation must be given; when an explanation has been given, people need to know what they can or should do. Information cannot be independent from the knowledge that is needed to use it. The more information, the better? In the past, when data was scarce, the assumption 'the more data, the more information' applied. These days, this is no longer the case, and the same assumption leads to an overabundance of data and an information blackout.

Knowledge

For centuries, philosophers, psychologists, logicians and many other sophisticates have been searching for the ultimate description of the concept of 'knowledge'. But even with all their knowledge (!) they could not define it conclusively. Since nobody knows exactly what it encompasses, making an issue out of it is not difficult. Practically every dictionary has a different definition of the concept of knowledge; the only thing we can conclude from this is that, indeed, knowledge is a subject that is difficult to describe.

In simple, generic terms: knowledge is information about the world that allows us to solve a problem.

The approximate approach of the concepts of data and information blocks our view of a clear description of what knowledge should represent. By way of a taster, for psychologists knowledge is the whole of the information a person (or more comprehensively, a group or a culture) possesses. Incidentally, cognitive psychology starts from the assumption that a human being is an information processing system. Given human nature, someone out there will disagree.

However, we can handle a relatively simple definition: knowledge is information about the world that allows us to do something. Knowledge allows us to transfer data to information, and to derive other information from that information. In other words, knowledge allows us to solve a problem.

Knowledge teaches us what is possible; experience teaches us what is impossible.

Working with knowledge means:

- Creating information (interpreting data)
- Using information (interpreting information) and re-using knowledge
- Disseminating information

Potential knowledge issues are:

- There is too much or not enough knowledge available
- Knowledge is not present at the right location
- The existing knowledge potential is unknown
- There are differences in meaning (content-wise, terminology-wise, quality-wise)
- Available knowledge is not easily accessible
- Knowledge cannot be maintained
- Etc.

Solving knowledge issues implies:

- Changes in the organisational-functional area:
    - re-organisation (structures, processes)
    - job upgrading/extension
    - formation, education, training
    - research and development
- Changes in the socio-cultural area (e.g. stimulating teamwork)
- Changes in the technical area (e.g. the introduction of *Decision Support Systems, Knowledge-based Systems or Expert Systems*)

Experience does not necessarily automatically lead to more knowledge; it's the combination of knowledge and experience that turns a specialist into an expert.

Your information and expertise count

Your information and expertise count and they are your biggest asset!

Organisations across all industries are becoming increasingly driven by their expertise and, more specifically, by the expertise of their knowledge workers.

This means that information, communication and knowledge are becoming significantly more important to support customers, to stay one step ahead of the competition, to innovate or to simply be efficient. The most important challenge for any organisation is to develop knowledge and keep it in the organisation.

Knowledge is not new

Epistemology

Who are we to define knowledge when, since Greek times, important philosophers and scientists have already been doing major brainwork on this subject and have been writing piles of books on it?

Epistemology is one of the main branches of philosophy and deals with the types, origin, objective and limitations of human knowledge. Epistemology is the real theory about knowledge.

Knowledge is linked to people

Although the wisdom and brainwork of philosophers such as Plato, Aristotle, Locke, Hume, Kant and Hegel apparently have little practical use in our modern society, it is a good thing to have knowledge of their concepts and angles.

For instance, Aristotle concluded that knowledge is something a person possesses, something in that person's mind or intellect.

Knowledge comes in different shapes and forms

Some thinkers, such as Bertrand Russell, argued that there are two types of knowledge. *Acquired knowledge* is based on direct experience and does not require justification.

The opposite, i.e. knowledge that is not based on direct experience, was called *knowledge by description*. It is justified to say that such information or knowledge can ultimately be reduced to someone's *acquired knowledge*.

That is why it is important to understand not only the content of information or knowledge; it is equally important to know the context of a knowledge element (object), the source, the objective.

Knowledge is a form of awareness and awakening

This proposition has been put forward by philosophers since the 5th century BC. Plato was the first to advance an extensive proposition on this. He considered knowledge as a mental status, closely related to – but different from – believing or having an opinion.

Other versions from those times considered knowledge as one element from a series of mental statuses that evolved with increasing certainty. This spectrum would start with guessing as the lowest level. They considered thinking, believing, and being certain of something as stronger forms of a conviction. Knowledge would be the highest level here.

Someone can possess knowledge without knowing it

Many 20th century philosophers reject the idea that knowledge is a mental status.

According to Wittgenstein, knowledge and certainty belong to different categories.

These philosophers accept the challenge to assign a deviant description or meaning to 'someone knows something, possesses knowledge'. They always start from the proposition that a person can possess knowledge without knowing it. They continue with arguments that it is wrong to assimilate forms of knowledge to forms of doubt, feeling pain, having an opinion/view on something.

The latter are mental statuses that a person is aware of. Therefore, 'someone can possess knowledge without knowing it'.

Someone who knows something possesses knowledge

We can distinguish two concepts of knowledge: tacit knowledge and available knowledge. Both forms result in the proposition that when a person knows something, that person possesses knowledge.

For instance, one of your colleagues is working on a problem and knows the solution. This colleague is aware of the solution and makes use of it. This colleague's knowledge is available – it has been applied in a given place at a given moment.

But that same colleague also possesses tacit knowledge. Currently, that colleague is not thinking about his/her address or about a given formula. But when someone asks about it, he/she can definitely give the answer. This is the concept of tacit knowledge – someone possesses knowledge without being explicitly aware of it at a given moment.

In both cases, we can say that this colleague knows something, or possesses knowledge.

Today's demanding knowledge economy

As a knowledge worker — sometimes even as an expert — I'm supposed to be *all-knowing* and *all-seeing*. Consequently, I nearly read myself to death to stay up-to-speed in my field. But people who only read specialist literature inevitably become narrow-minded and narrow-minded people don't make good professionals. It's far more enriching also to keep an eye on developments in related, or even completely unrelated, fields. This implies even more reading, even more 'information processing' (for convenience's sake, I don't use the term 'information management' just yet).

Ordinary people who have been living in caves for the past few years don't have a clue, but knowledge workers and experts like us know that indeed 'something' is going on. Concepts such as *information overload, information explosion, information overkill, information inundation, information monster, information obesity, information dirt, info glut, info bog, info garbage, info glitz, info glimmer, info pollution, data smog, data deluge, data glut, information fatigue syndrome, information anxiety,* and maybe even *information underload* — the feeling that everything you know is worthless — are quiet evidence of it.

The information society in which we live expects us to increase our knowledge endlessly and improve performance. Whilst it was easy to keep an up-to-date, general view of your field 10 to 15 years ago, these days we are faced with an increasing volume of information and knowledge.

Some people claim they can remember everything. But if we are honest, it is unrealistic to expect of ourselves, and definitely of others, to remember everything.

How much time do we lose due to un-productivity related to information?
How many times do we have to end our search without finding the (right) answer?
What do we do with all those emails?
Why do I keep writing down the same stuff?
Have you experienced information stress?
Do you drown in the sheer volume of data?
Do you lose time searching for information?
Are you also facing piles of reading material in order to 'stay up-to-date'?

INFORMATION OVERLOAD

There is no universal definition of 'information overload', but we can assume that information overload originates when someone:

- ▷ Doesn't understand the available information
- ▷ Feels taken by surprise by the quantity of information to understand
- ▷ Doesn't know whether certain information exists
- ▷ Doesn't know where to look for certain information
- ▷ Knows where to look for certain information, but doesn't have access to it
- ▷ Doesn't know whether information is reliable

Apart from the physical and mental problems (just think of the *'Information Fatigue Syndrome'*, described by David Lewis of the *International Stress Management Association*) information overload may cause; it really is a problem, certainly in organisations, since it leads to:

- ▷ Wasted time
- ▷ Poor decision-making
- ▷ The inability to find quality in the quantity

And that's not all (things will only get worse before they get better); the use of modern technologies simplifies information distribution even more, while technological evolution has not yet reached its end by a long way.

***Information anxiety* is the black hole between data and knowledge, the difference between the things that people understand, and the things that they think they should understand.**

We do have to ask ourselves what we are doing, though; half of the world's population lives on less than a euro a day and has never used a telephone, let alone the internet.

Knowledge issues

Knowledge allows us to transfer data to information, and to derive other information from that information. In other words, knowledge allows us to solve a problem.

*Knowledge teaches us what is possible;
experience teaches us what is impossible.*

Working with knowledge means:

- Creating validated, context-enriched information (as knowledge representation)
- Using information (interpreting information) and re-using knowledge
- Disseminating information

Potential knowledge issues are:

- There is too much information and not enough knowledge available
- Knowledge is not present in the right location
- The existing knowledge potential is unknown
- There are differences in meaning (content-wise, terminology-wise, quality-wise)
- Available knowledge is not easily accessible
- Knowledge cannot be maintained
- Etc.

Solving knowledge issues implies:

- Changes in the organisational-functional area:
  - re-organisation (structures, processes, time allowances)
  - example role of top management
  - job upgrading/extension
  - formation, education, training
  - research and development

- ▷ Changes in the socio-cultural area (e.g. stimulating teamwork)
- ▷ Changes in the technical area (e.g. the introduction of *Decision Support Systems, Knowledge-based Systems* or *Expert Systems*)

Experience does not necessarily automatically lead to more knowledge; rather, it's the combination of knowledge and experience that turns a specialist into an expert.

What international studies say

On managing documents

Gartner (paper and documents)
- ▷ The average document is copied, either physically or electronically, nine to 11 times at a cost of about €18
- ▷ Documents cost about €20 to file
- ▷ Retrieving a misfiled document costs about €120
- ▷ 80% to 95% of enterprise information is located within paper and electronic documents
- ▷ 25% of enterprise documents are misplaced and will never be located again
- ▷ 30% of Gartner Group clients store more than 50% of their documents on local hard drives or USB sticks
- ▷ Document mismanagement claims:
  - ▷ 40% to 60% of office workers' time
  - ▷ 20% to 45% of labour costs
  - ▷ 2% to 15% of corporate revenue

Topic	Improvement
Time savings with regard to creating and modifying documents	50%-90%
Increase in productivity	20%-30%
Savings on document handling	20%-40%
Improvements in cycle time	20%-40%
Savings on disk space	30%-50%
Improvements in customer satisfaction	30%-50%

Arbeidsgemeinschaft für wirtschaftliche Verwaltung (AWV) (potential improvements)

On finding information

Time spent searching per person, of knowledge workers	9.6	Hours per week

IDC, the expanding universe (2002)

Poor decisions based on faulty or poor information	
Duplicated efforts within different divisions/projects	
Lost sales due to customers' inability to find product or services	
Lost productivity due to employees' inability to find information	
% of searches resulting in NO answer (hence, need for expert locator)	40%
% of search time spent looking for external sources	16%
Time spent searching per person, of knowledge workers	13.3 35% of productive time

IDC, the high cost of not finding information (2004)

Time spent searching per person	Hours per week	
>8	29%	
6-8	13%	
4-6	31%	
2-4	19%	
<2	8%	
Weighted average	5.72	Hours per week
% of an organisation's knowledge stored in the heads of its staff	42%	

Delphi Consulting Group, survey

Conclusions:
- ▷ 35% of productive time is spent searching, per person (for knowledge workers)
- ▷ 40% of searches result in NO answer (hence, need for an expert locator)
- ▷ 16% of search time is spent looking for external sources
- ▷ 42% of an organisation's knowledge is stored in the heads of its staff

On email

% of staff losing important email	22%
% of staff spending four hours a day on email	41%

YouGov, survey

% of staff issues with regard to finding email	65%
% of staff issues with regard to managing email	51%
% of staff issues with regard to too much CC email	39%
% of staff issues with regard to legal value (litigation) of email	28%
% of staff issues with regard to performance of email server	20%
% of staff issues with regard to compliance and regulations	15%
% of staff issues with regard to personal email archive	14%
% of staff issues with regard to cost of email	9%
% of staff issues with regard to duplicated email	7%

Computable Nl, survey

% of IT managers seeing email anarchy as a problem	81%
% of IT managers seeing email archiving as a problem	78%
% of UK IT managers seeing email archiving as a problem	90%

MORI uk, survey

OPPORTUNITIES FOR IMPROVEMENT

Recession?

Every time the economy stagnates, companies focus on the preservation or an improvement of the company results. There are various ways of increasing profit. Increased sales efforts and a sharper purchase policy are just two examples.

In most cases, people are put under pressure to work harder and more productively. Many are frustrated and stressed by the difference between their personal efforts and the organisation's inefficiency concerning information management and the flow of this information throughout the organisation.

The majority of enterprises do not opt for measures that lead to a more effective, efficient use and organisation of information and knowledge, be it in times of economic recession or boom.

Undoing positive efforts

All too often, people forget that many positive efforts are lost because they lose time searching for the right information, in the right quantity. People do not know who they can turn to for a quick and accurate answer and questions answered previously are answered again and again.

Running into a brick wall

Meanwhile, in most organisations, company results are under pressure once again and people rightly ask themselves if there are any hidden losses standing in the way of (higher) profits.

Unstructured information and knowledge make up 80% of the information and knowledge in an organisation. Today, companies focus their investments mainly on accounting, ERP and CRM applications, which are restricted to the 20% structured data in their organisation. Hence, there is a whole new opportunity for better company results if organisations addressed the remaining 80% of information.

In our personal environment — at home and at work — things are exactly the same: a personal organiser, databases for all kinds of numbers. But the information problem or the knowledge problem has never been recognised or dealt with.

Quotes from Leading People

"In a world with physical limits, it is discoveries of big ideas together with the discovery of millions of little ideas that make persistent economic growth possible."

Paul Romer
(1993)

"Knowledge, during the last few decades, has become the central capital, the cost centre and the crucial resource of the economy."

Peter Drucker
(1969)

"Knowledge is our most powerful engine of production; it enables us to subdue nature and force her to satisfy our wants. Organisation aids knowledge."

Marshall
(1920)

"The only thing that gives an organisation a competitive edge is... what it knows, how it uses what it knows and how fast it can know something new."

Larry Prusak
(1996)

"Economists have always recognised the dominant role that increasing knowledge and information plays in economic processes, but have, for the most part, found the whole subject of knowledge and information too slippery to handle..."

Edith Penrose
(1959)

Knowledge from a management perspective

Still not convinced about the value and urgency of appropriate management of your knowledge? Or is it just another hype for you?

Maybe you are right! Maybe Scott Simon's quote applies to you: 'Intelligent people can always come up with intelligent reasons to do nothing.'

For sure, Knowledge Management is NOT about managing knowledge. Knowledge Management is more about managing organisations from a different perspective.

A number of practical considerations are elaborated further in the next chapter.

And imagine the following in your organisation:

▷ Decisions taken without correct information and knowledge
▷ Risks detected without knowledge and context
▷ Innovation-driven without appropriate market and technological knowledge
▷ Helping your clients without knowledge of their business

Personal experiences and reflections

Is there really a need for Knowledge Management in your organisation?

What is data, information or knowledge?

▷ Facebook discussions with friends
▷ Twitter messages
▷ BI SQL statements
▷ A complaint on a product
▷ An invoice
▷ Collection of business cards

List your most important business reasons on initiating or continuing with Information and Knowledge Management.

Have a look on www.knowliah.eu/kcm/2 for other questions, ideas, discussion and answers on this topic.

My lessons learned

The following is a collection of independent topics I learned during the last 12 years spent on Knowledge Management and related topics.

ON INFORMATION AND KNOWLEDGE

Accept chaos

I have to admit, being an engineer by education, that it took me four years to accept that there will always be chaos, even in organisations.

To structure everything and maintain it in a proper way is not achievable. The main practical reasons for this are:

People act differently

First of all, not all human beings deal with information in the same structured way. In each organisation, you will find people with a flat list of files in their My Documents. Others are overacting and have structures of 15 levels and more.

Secondly, people are not consistent when it comes to structuring information. One day they put information at the top level (flat-list type); the next day they put it five or six levels deep in a folder structure. And what is probably more dangerous, some will classify the same information, on different occasions and on different days, in different locations in a tree structure.

Not worth managing

Not all information is sufficiently valuable to be structured. Structuring information – and maintaining it – takes time and effort and requires a type of quality control. Why would you make that investment for information with a low value to the organisation?

One can argue: *'We don't know the value of information or knowledge, so we have to structure everything'*. This is a valid argument and the wrong conclusion. Make sure you discover which information and knowledge is valuable to your organisation.

Volumes

When it comes to internal information and knowledge, an organisation with sufficient profit margins may be able to structure everything and avoid chaos. However, as a shareholder of that company, I would prefer another use of that profit.

The volume of relevant external information is as big as the volume of relevant internal information. Very few organisations have the vision and the means to appoint people responsible for integrating this in the organisation in a structured way.

And what about the things that are only stored in your colleagues' heads?

Value defines the effort

From the previous point, it is clear that the value of an information or knowledge entity defines the effort an organisation will invest in capturing, structuring and maintaining it.

From practical experience, the value is composed of four dimensions:

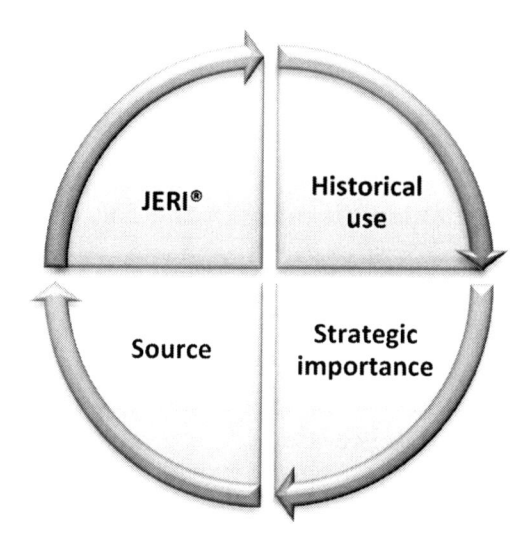

(Diagram: JERI® — Historical use, Strategic importance, Source)

Historical use

80% of your internal information is almost never used. Would you make an effort if you know the document, report, innovation, etc. will not be used?

Strategic importance

Within this 80% of hardly-used information and knowledge, you have a set of legally and strategically important elements, e.g. contracts, invoices, strategic reports, new laws and regulations etc.

Source

Who is the author? Who reviewed and approved? How are users quoting the content? And most importantly, until when is the information usable? When was it last maintained?

Those are all indicators of the quality of the content.

JERI®

JERI® is short for Just Enough Relevant Information, when and where needed. You will learn more on JERI® later in this chapter.

How well is an organisation capable of delivering JERI® to its collaborators? Information and knowledge might be very useful and valuable, but not when your organisation is not capable of delivering the right information and knowledge to the right person at the right moment.

More on this in the section 'JERI®'.

Securing versus securing

Securing has a double meaning in the context of Knowledge Management:

- ▷ Securing as in protecting and limiting access to specific information and knowledge
- ▷ Securing as in capturing information and knowledge, saving it for later re-use

Securing (protecting) knowledge may seem to be the opposite of sharing knowledge. However, it is a tough and under-recognised subject in large organisations with a shifting production towards BRICS countries. Securing is then a secret and omnipresent subject.

Securing (capturing) knowledge is quickly pronounced and slowly implemented. Experts need to be trained and coached when it comes to the structuring, enriching with context, writing and reviewing towards a target audience, of their valuable knowledge.

More on this in the topic 'Sharing knowledge?'

Another frontier

In the last two decades, our information world changed dramatically. In today's information- and knowledge-driven economy – almost without noticing – it is not about internal or external information any more. External information is almost as accessible as internal information.

The new frontier is not your organisation, but the distinction between validated and non-validated information and knowledge. In the past, publishers took care to validate content and publish it in respectable books. With the internet, most people believe presented information is correct and validated by experts.

So, you need to draw your frontier between validated (trusted) sources and non-validated ones. Most knowledge workers tend to forget or neglect this new frontier.

Quality of information and knowledge

Low quality of information in an enterprise repository is a demotivator for Knowledge and Information Management.

Quality is reflected in:

- ▷ The use of templates (lay-out and document structures)
- ▷ Language and terminology used (oriented towards the target audience)
- ▷ Revisions, maintenance and approvals by appropriate experts

ON PEOPLE AND CHANGE

People's heads

People's heads are different on the outside. Nobody would argue with this. But people's heads are different on the inside as well!

Not that our brain has a physically different 'face'. However, we all received a different education, we were raised in a different environment, have different interests, have different experiences in other organisations, etc. All those elements have ensured that our brain interconnections (synapses, cortex) were built – and are continuing to be built – in a quite different way.

This personal 'internal face' makes us act differently when it comes to:

▷ Classifying information
▷ Presenting information in folder structures
▷ Explaining problems or solutions to each other
▷ Structuring our knowledge
▷ Assessing risks
▷ Making decisions
▷ Accepting change

Knowledge Management programmes that do not respect this 'internal face' of individuals are not doomed to fail, but the probability of success is much, much lower.

Who is an expert?

Everybody and nobody. Everybody possesses knowledge, expertise and wisdom. The question and challenge is to identify, match and feed personal knowledge with the knowledge required by the organisation in order to be successful.

Nobody is an expert as long as the personal knowledge is not used and applied for the sake of organisational results.

Knowledge Management is not about experts, or about collecting knowledge, or about developing personal knowledge. It is about *respecting* the expert for *his/her contribution* to the organisation.

Sharing knowledge?

I walk away when a manager tells me, "My people have to share their knowledge." The objective of Knowledge Management is NOT sharing knowledge. Rather, it is a result thereof.

Or even worse... When a CEO or other manager introduces Knowledge Management as 'a programme to share knowledge' to the collaborators, you can be sure this organisation will not achieve any Knowledge Management result in the next two years. People – at a personal level – see an obligation to share their knowledge as a real threat to their job. When threatened, humans go into defensive mode. In this case, it means they will protect their knowledge even more. Correcting this logical reaction and attitude will take a couple of years.

Communicate personal benefit

Employee support is an essential element in every implementation or (positive) change. It can be achieved through:

- A consensus about its necessity
- The fact that employees are the requesting party
- An inquiry round (people will feel involved)
- Dealing with 'their' problems
- 'A say' and involvement in the phasing of the solution
- 'A say' and involvement in the elaboration of the solution (people will recognise 'their' problems)

The foundation of all improvements — hence, changes — for a user is his or her personal benefit. When users do not see a direct or indirect personal benefit, they will not be inclined to contribute to change or put in the extra effort.

Management by example

When management is convinced that knowledge, information and documents are an important ingredient and growth factor for any organisation, it is strongly recommended to incorporate this into personal and team targets.

This way, it can become an evaluation criterion during the (half-) yearly appraisal and employees can be tackled about it. However, try to avoid translating it into financial benefits. Instead, translate it into recognition and respect as an employee becomes an expert in a given domain.

As a parent, you play the role of example for your children. In much the same way, management (of each level) is an example for its team, department or organisation. So, make sure your words and actions point in the same direction. Many Knowledge Management initiatives fail because this obvious and simple rule was not respected.

Never forget the following saying by Confucius:

'I don't understand what you say, because what you say and what you do is different.'

Organisational framework

This entity is contained in the organisational framework that reflects the context (and division) of the organisation. In today's organisations, this is no longer a matrix structure, but a multi-dimensional unit with the following important dimensions:

- ▷ The business processes in the organisation requiring information and knowledge
- ▷ The products, projects and services (both inflow and outflow)
- ▷ Hierarchy, departments and committees
- ▷ Specific (technical) knowledge domains

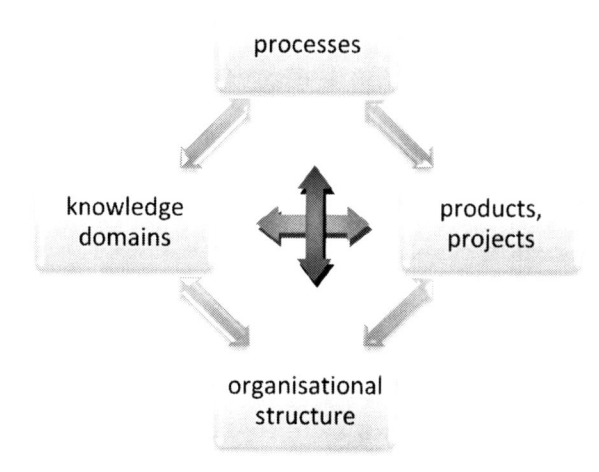

processes

knowledge domains

products, projects

organisational structure

Knowledge domains

Knowledge domains can be divided into smaller entities.

An example of the application of a traditional classification system in the context of Knowledge Management is the WIIG system (from 1993).

WIIG foresees different levels for categorising information:

- knowledge domain
- knowledge region
- knowledge section

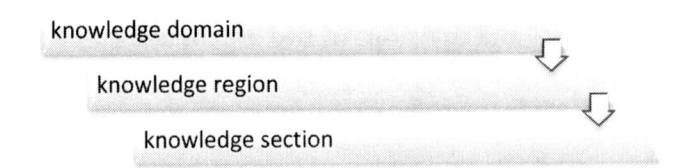

And you can continue with:

▷ Knowledge segment
▷ Knowledge element
▷ Knowledge fragment
▷ Knowledge atom

Let's use kidney diseases as an example. We all know someone who drinks or eats too much, don't we?

Category	Example
Knowledge domain	Internal medicine
Knowledge region	Urology
Knowledge section	Kidney diseases
Knowledge segment	Diagnoses of kidney diseases
Knowledge element	Diagnostic strategies
Knowledge fragment	If the symptom is excruciating pain, then consider kidney stone
Knowledge atom	Excruciating pain is a symptom

ON KNOWLEDGE MANAGEMENT ITSELF

Different for each organisation

There is no such thing as a universal definition or implementation plan for Knowledge Management.

The complexity of the subject, the unique character of each organisation, its people and activities make Knowledge Management different for each organisation.

Nevertheless, in the last part of this book we describe a potential pragmatic approach that fits each organisation.

Further in this book, you will also find a rough implementation plan. 'Rough' because it requires specific adaptations for each organisation.

Much more than just ICT

Knowledge Management is much more than an ICT initiative; it involves four different domains. In fact, each ICT initiative should be approached from those four domains:

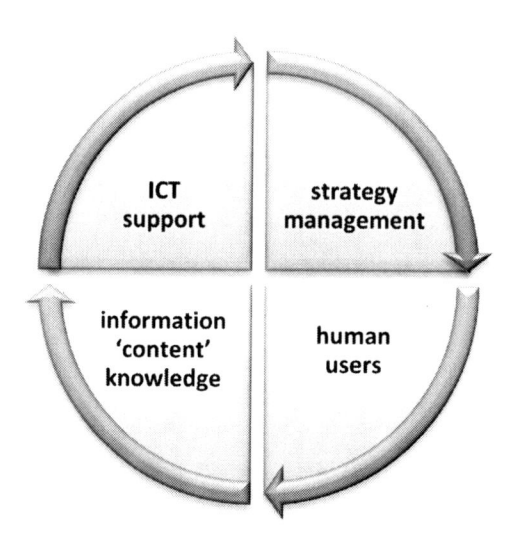

- ICT support
- strategy management
- information 'content' knowledge
- human users

Strategy – Management

Knowledge Management requires a business-aligned strategy and continuous management support. You risk ending up with some isolated initiatives, requiring a lot of energy and budgets without the expected results.

Human users

No happy users, no results.

More than other programmes, a Knowledge Management programme requires maximum support and contribution from the user/knowledge worker, both in his/her role as knowledge supplier and as knowledge consumer.

Content

No qualitative and clear content, no results.

Content is the carrier of information and knowledge between people. It is all about communication between people using the right wording, templates, targeted to an audience. Outdated or poisoned information will scare off users.

ICT support

And of course – having the previous three points sorted out – you need to choose the right ICT support (and not the other way round, as it is usually done).

Knowledge Management involves communication

Communication is the transfer of information between the location where the information originates and the point of receipt, without a change in form, content or order.

Hence, the *communication process* consists of a sender (of the information), a message (the information) and a receiver (of the information). The process is concluded by a feedback process for the communicated message.

As people, we communicate with other people, directly or via information carriers. Every form of communication is based on words, terms. Every word has its own definition as well as its own context in which it is used. Standardising *terminology* and making it unambiguous results in clearer information and less risk of communication and interpretation errors.

Writing is more than simply translating thoughts into written language; it is a process that involves different factors. Writing is also the skill that helps to get this mental process going and structure it.

A *template* is a set of page and style definitions. This predefined set (a .dot file in Microsoft Word) allows you to format (design) different documents in exactly the same way without having to manually format or modify each paragraph.

Privacy

Privacy is a difficult subject in the context of Knowledge Management.

'Who uses what?' and 'Who knows what?' can be seen as having a (limited) impact on an individual's personal sphere.

However, privacy as a subject is often exaggerated. People do not have issues with:

- ▷ Time registrations
- ▷ Details for HR purposes
- ▷ A personal profile on an intranet
- ▷ The use of public communities like Facebook, Twitter, LinkedIn, Ecademy, Plaxo, etc.
- ▷ Telling all their private details to their colleagues

Privacy is not a '*fait-divers*' and needs to be placed in its correct context with regard to Knowledge Management.

Content

The presence or absence of valuable content will entail the success or failure of a Knowledge Management programme.

Finding answers with relevant content during a first visit will encourage users to further use and adopt a new Knowledge Management way of working.

Quality of content and a minimum critical mass have frequently been the first steps towards successful Knowledge Management initiatives in organisations.

Time allowance

When knowledge creation is part of the job, it is also *much clearer* to the experts and management that time and effort can and must be spent on answering questions and securing these answers in validated knowledge objects.

Especially in a start-up phase, employees must be allowed time for the creation, maintenance and enrichment of *validated high-quality information* (as a knowledge representation). Employees cannot record and share their information and knowledge with their colleagues if they are not allowed the necessary time to do so.

Promote re-use!

Instead of sending out the message to share knowledge, management should promote the re-use of each other's valuable information and knowledge.

In practice, it is the lack of re-use (and related respect) that limits the results of Knowledge Management, not the willingness to share knowledge.

Re-use is not just making a copy, re-use encompasses different levels:

- Direct - the information or knowledge object is directly re-usable for your context
- Indirect - the information or knowledge object needs reworking before being re-usable for your context
- Background - the information or knowledge object provides relevant background information or earlier experiences for your case

JERI®

In the last 10 years, JERI® has almost become my second name.

The challenge today is not to collect information; the current technological tools have made that fairly easy. The big challenge is JERI® — *'Just Enough Relevant Information*, when you need it'.

PERSONAL EXPERIENCES AND REFLECTIONS

Is it smart/safe/stupid/harmful/productive to:

- ▷ Make extra copies of important documents for personal usage?
- ▷ Throw away archives of documents?
- ▷ Throw away archives of emails?
- ▷ Build an information warehouse?
- ▷ Push people to share knowledge?
- ▷ Focus on the objectives of the management?

Have a look on www.knowliah.eu/kcm/3 for other questions, ideas, discussion and answers on this topic.

Retrieving and delivering only that information which is relevant in the context of the moment is the aim.

This JERI® concept is applicable on all levels: personal, in teams, departments, organisations, even for the government and media.

KNOWLEDGE LOGISTICS

Overview

Knowledge also goes through a logistic process of creation, storage and management, communication, use, maintenance, recycling and so on.

Every phase and step is essentially aimed at creating value for your organisational knowledge.

A logical set-up would be:

▷ Determining your mission and objectives with regard to Knowledge Management: where do you want to be in five years' time, what does this mean in terms of objectives in three years' time, in two years' time and in one year's time (thinking back from the future)?

▷ What do we have, what is needed, what can only be found in people's heads?

▷ How can we capture, test and validate missing or hidden knowledge?

▷ Using our knowledge and information optimally (in different forms) leads to the actual creation of value for our information, knowledge and expertise

▷ On the basis of use, concentrations and evolutions, evaluate how the creation of content and value can be further optimised

The total knowledge logistics framework can be represented as follows:

KM ACTIVITIES AND PROCESSES
(H. VAN HEGHE)

mission (organisation → knowledge, information, communication)	
objectives	strategy

inventory		
available	needed	hidden

content creation		
development	purchase	partners

value creation			
sharing	learning	applying	re-using

directing	
evaluation (creation, value, etc.)	discovery of evolution

continuous

Knowledge sources

Do you have a clear overview of the internal and external knowledge sources needed by the various departments of your organisation?

The main knowledge sources are:

- ▷ Validated and tested information
- ▷ Respected experts
- ▷ External (re)sources
- ▷ Analysed data (BI reports)
- ▷ Graphics, multi-media

Each one of your knowledge sources has related logistic knowledge processes (see further) and needs its own specific processes for knowledge creation, capturing and maintenance.

HUMAN COMPETENCES

If it does at all, how does your organisation distinguish between technical competences, management skills, etc.?

A traditional division is:

▷ Knowledge
▷ Attitude
▷ Behaviour

An alternative, more suitable division in this context would be:

▷ Instrumental   (what, knowledge)
▷ Intermediate   (how, processes)
▷ Transitional   (why, leadership, behaviour)

Knowledge about Knowledge Management

PERSONAL EXPERIENCES AND REFLECTIONS

Add more potential elements on:

- ▷ KM preparation and know-how
- ▷ KM context and supporting areas
- ▷ Knowledge Worker perspective
- ▷ Knowledge Organisation perspective

Have a look on www.knowliah.eu/kcm/4 for other questions, ideas, discussion and answers on this topic.

Overview

As one scheme, it results in:

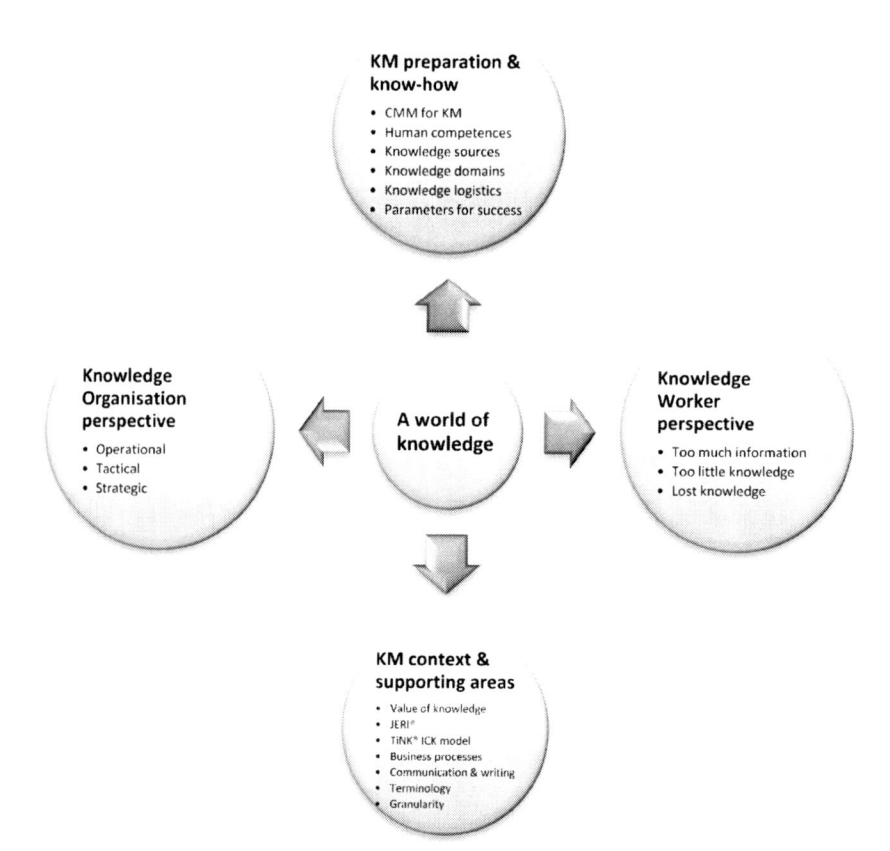

KM preparation & know-how
- CMM for KM
- Human competences
- Knowledge sources
- Knowledge domains
- Knowledge logistics
- Parameters for success

Knowledge Organisation perspective
- Operational
- Tactical
- Strategic

A world of knowledge

Knowledge Worker perspective
- Too much information
- Too little knowledge
- Lost knowledge

KM context & supporting areas
- Value of knowledge
- JERI®
- TiNK® ICK model
- Business processes
- Communication & writing
- Terminology
- Granularity

Knowledge organisation perspective

As a management member of a knowledge organisation, your main concern is a totally different aspect of Knowledge Management.

Operational results

Are business processes carried out correctly and expertly? Are we sufficiently productive? Do we attain the right level of service? Do we use the right communication for the right target groups (internally and externally)?

Tactical component

Do we know enough to make the right decisions? Do we know enough to assess potential risks correctly? What about our quality? How do the market and our competitors evolve? Do we meet regulations (compliance)? How do we deal with ideas and innovation?

Strategic elements

What do we know? What don't we know? Which knowledge is used the most and is therefore needed? How does our knowledge evolve? Where are the knowledge risks? What do we need to know tomorrow?

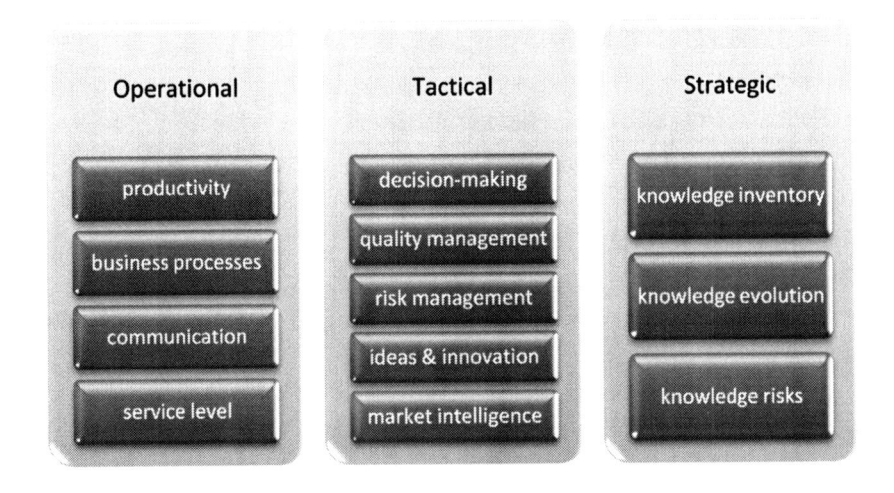

Operational	Tactical	Strategic
productivity	decision-making	knowledge inventory
business processes	quality management	
communication	risk management	knowledge evolution
service level	ideas & innovation	knowledge risks
	market intelligence	

Knowledge worker perspective

The knowledge worker in your organisation only wants an answer to three crucial knowledge phenomena:

Too much information

'We are drowning in information...' Everyone is drowning in the information overload. We search through the enormous volume, but we do not find. Around 42% to 50% of searches result in an unsuitable answer or no answer at all! Does your organisation provide sufficient support for the knowledge worker?

Too little knowledge

'... and starving for knowledge.' The hunger for knowledge. The right knowledge at the right moment. Sufficient basic knowledge for a correct interpretation of the information. Advice from a colleague for that other light...

Lost knowledge

Reorganisations, retirements, staff turnover. Gone is the colleague I could always turn to for an explanation.

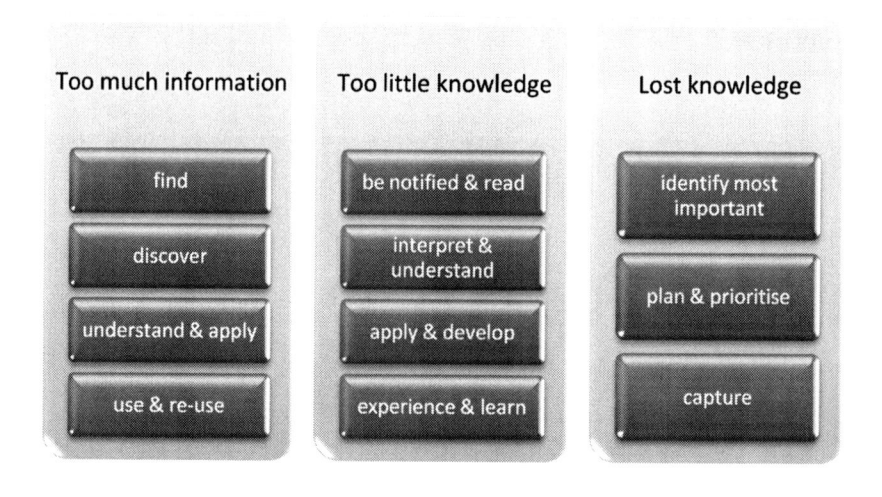

Too much information	Too little knowledge	Lost knowledge
find	be notified & read	identify most important
discover	interpret & understand	plan & prioritise
understand & apply	apply & develop	capture
use & re-use	experience & learn	

Have your knowledge workers learned how to write? Not just putting down letters on paper, but transmitting a message or an essence to a target audience.

Terminology

15% of your knowledge is contained in words – the basis of human communication.

How does your organisation deal with definitions, synonyms, translations – fine-tuning and use?

Information granularity

Information – and also knowledge – should not be considered as one big unit, an encyclopaedia. Division into smaller independent entities is a necessary condition for efficient and effective application and re-use.

The Knowledge Management building blocks

Knowledge Management is not an isolated phenomenon, but the most important cornerstone of our knowledge economy, sustained entrepreneurship, intellectual challenges and good management.

Knowledge value

The value of information and knowledge is determined by four or so parameters. Value is an important decision-making parameter. Why would you or your employees invest time and energy in the 80% of information and knowledge that is never used? Can you identify this 80% in your organisation?

JERI® – Just Enough Relevant Information/knowledge, when and where needed

For the best results on the basis of your expertise, you yourself, your colleagues and your entire organisation need JERI®. No piles of information or terabytes on a server, but 'Just Enough Relevant Information', when and where needed.

Context and model

To be able to achieve JERI® for the knowledge worker, you need two elements:

- ▷ An information model on the basis of contextual enrichment (for instance, the TiNK® method)
- ▷ Set-up of the user's profile on the basis of this information model

Business processes

Daily tasks may or may not be carried out on the basis of business processes. But have the information and knowledge that are needed to carry out the process correctly been taken sufficiently into account in these processes? Which information and knowledge is created that can be useful for another knowledge player?

Communication and writing

Communities, portals, messaging, email… How does your organisation deal with the different communication methods and platforms in an efficient way? What do you use where?

members of the management will not be happy about: shielding off information and knowledge becomes visible, missing knowledge and expertise becomes visible, potentially there is less space for 'irrelevant' sidesteps.

This often leads to resistance or, in some cases, even to sabotage. Take this into account in time and give it the appropriate attention.

Knowledge about Knowledge Management

Before you as an organisation can start with Knowledge Management, you need to acquire sufficient know-how on Knowledge Management – the 'do's and don'ts' – on the preparation and on meeting the necessary conditions:

CMM for Knowledge Management

The Capability Maturity Model for Knowledge Management is a framework that allows you to evaluate where you are as a knowledge organisation and where you want to be in four years' time. As such, it represents a possible evolution from a Knowledge-Chaotic organisation to a Knowledge-Centred organisation with possible intermediate steps.

Human competences

If it does at all, how does your organisation distinguish between technical competences, management skills, etc.?

Knowledge sources

Do you have a clear overview of the internal and external knowledge sources needed by the various departments of your organisation?

Knowledge logistics

Knowledge also goes through a logistic process of creation, storage and management, communication, use, maintenance, recycling.

Parameters for success

Typical mistakes with regard to Knowledge Management are usually situated in the human or organisational area. Have these been sufficiently addressed?

Knowledge domains

Which knowledge domains are relevant for your organisation? Today? Tomorrow? The day after that? Who are the 'champions' for each of these domains?

Knowledge Management risks

Knowledge Management in your organisation will also entail a number of changes and may have consequences that (certain)

A WORLD OF KNOWLEDGE

The Knowledge Management framework is a framework that helps people to acquire know-how on Knowledge Management.

This framework is based on over 10 years of experience with Knowledge Management, with more than 100 customers in all sectors, SMEs to enterprises, public and private sector.

As such, it gives a face to Knowledge Management and provides a pragmatic way forward to becoming a knowledge-centred organisation. The framework focuses on four crucial domains:

- KM preparation & know-how
- Knowledge Organisation perspective
- A world of knowledge
- Knowledge Worker perspective
- KM context & supporting areas

In a number of cases (e.g. Wegeman), the knowledge organisation perspective is referred to as the inside-out approach and the knowledge worker perspective as an outside-in approach.

Knowledge Management framework

PART II

A Knowledge Management framework

This section discusses a practical framework on Knowledge Management.

As such, it will help you to:

- ▷ Learn and understand more about Knowledge Management and its linked elements
- ▷ Position the different components of Knowledge Management in the right perspective
- ▷ Help you to define your objectives and approach to Knowledge Management

Sharing knowledge?

I walk away when a manager tells me, "My people have to share their knowledge." The objective of Knowledge Management is NOT sharing knowledge. Rather, it is a result thereof.

Or even worse... When a CEO or other manager introduces Knowledge Management as 'a programme to share knowledge' to the collaborators, you can be sure this organisation will not achieve any Knowledge Management result in the next two years. People – at a personal level – see an obligation to share their knowledge as a real threat to their job. When threatened, humans go into defensive mode. In this case, it means they will protect their knowledge even more. Correcting this logical reaction and attitude will take a couple of years.

Communicate personal benefit

Employee support is an essential element in every implementation or (positive) change. It can be achieved through:

- ▷ A consensus about its necessity
- ▷ The fact that employees are the requesting party
- ▷ An inquiry round (people will feel involved)
- ▷ Dealing with 'their' problems
- ▷ 'A say' and involvement in the phasing of the solution
- ▷ 'A say' and involvement in the elaboration of the solution (people will recognise 'their' problems)

The foundation of all improvements — hence, changes — for a user is his or her personal benefit. When users do not see a direct or indirect personal benefit, they will not be inclined to contribute to change or put in the extra effort.

Management by example

When management is convinced that knowledge, information and documents are an important ingredient and growth factor for any organisation, it is strongly recommended to incorporate this into personal and team targets.

This way, it can become an evaluation criterion during the (half-) yearly appraisal and employees can be tackled about it. However, try to avoid translating it into financial benefits. Instead, translate it into recognition and respect as an employee becomes an expert in a given domain.

As a parent, you play the role of example for your children. In much the same way, management (of each level) is an example for its team, department or organisation. So, make sure your words and actions point in the same direction. Many Knowledge Management initiatives fail because this obvious and simple rule was not respected.

Never forget the following saying by Confucius:

'I don't understand what you say, because what you say and what you do is different.'

Logistic process

The micro framework of an information/knowledge entity or subject can be represented as follows:

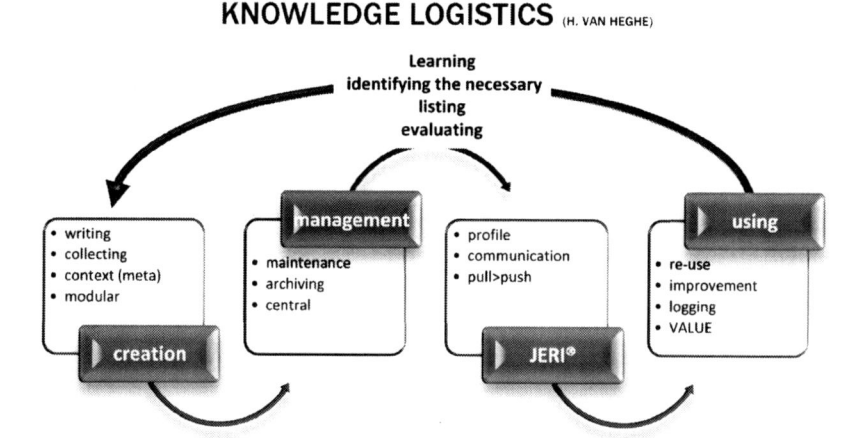

KNOWLEDGE LOGISTICS (H. VAN HEGHE)

Learning
identifying the necessary
listing
evaluating

- **creation**
  - writing
  - collecting
  - context (meta)
  - modular
- **management**
  - maintenance
  - archiving
  - central
- **JERI®**
  - profile
  - communication
  - pull>push
- **using**
  - re-use
  - improvement
  - logging
  - VALUE

Creation

The creation process consists of generating knowledge within the organisation. The organisation can undertake different activities and initiatives to increase its knowledge stock by:

▷ Fusion with another organisation or department
▷ Fusion of activities
▷ R&D activities
▷ Informal networks

Contextual enrichment is crucial in order to achieve JERI®.

Modular (i.e. smaller) parts make information more accessible and more re-usable.

Management

The collection and coding of knowledge consists mainly of identifying that specific knowledge in the information flow that is important for the organisation and making it accessible in a simple way, i.e. explicit, ordered, understandable and 'transferable'.

IT systems mainly use taxonomies for coding content to make subsequent retrieval 'a piece of cake'.

The objective of taxonomy is simplifying:

- The physical storage of the document thanks to the assignment of metadata
- The retrieval of these electronic documents thanks to the use of the same metadata
- The notification on periodical maintenance of information is crucial. Information too has a 'freshness date' and a 'use-by date'

JERI®

JERI® = the ultimate objective to support the knowledge worker

JERI® = Just Enough Relevant Information, when and where needed

It implies a mapping between user profiles and information and knowledge profiles. In turn, this leads to a lot less PUSH, but a lot more PULL of relevant information.

The corporate culture should especially encourage the re-use of knowledge through the creation of an environment in which employees share their knowledge.

Use

In order to promote intelligent re-use of knowledge, an organisation must create a number of mechanisms:

- JERI®
- Allowing time for knowledge targets to be reached
- Providing access to structural knowledge and referring to existing sources
- Establishing quality procedures to ensure a solid basis of reliable, complete knowledge, simple in use and with added value
- Training and coaching of employees with regard to the use, modification and deployment of the intellectual means of the organisation

Use and security

Mechanisms aimed at protecting knowledge. Four types of checks are mostly applied here:

▷ **Legal protection:** as legislation differs from country to country, the set-up can be difficult; in practice, mostly a non-compete clause in the employment contract of the employee, a clause that must not be too restrictive but that must protect the real importance of the organisation at the same time

▷ **Social mechanisms:** the organisation sets the boundaries with regard to knowledge sharing: what can be shared? who is the owner of the knowledge?

▷ **Structural mechanisms:** 'locking' knowledge in procedures, in the systems and products of the organisation – if the competition wants to copy these, they not only need to acquire the knowledge, but also the employees who possess this know-how and who are up-to-date with regard to internal team relations, etc.

▷ **Logging:** (often a difficult subject, but also the most sensible solution) recording who consults and communicates which information/knowledge

Learning

In a learning organisation in the knowledge field, we distinguish four points of attention:

▷ Identifying required knowledge
  ▷ which knowledge do we need?
  ▷ today? tomorrow? the day after tomorrow?
▷ Creating an inventory of the current knowledge
  ▷ which knowledge do we have?
  ▷ which knowledge is missing? which is superfluous?
  ▷ what is the **knowledge evolution** like?

- Evaluating value
  - how is the knowledge/information used?
  - how to maintain it? what is valuable?
  - who contributes?
- Learning at different levels in the organisation
  - individually, my own lessons learned
  - at team level, reflection within a group
  - at organisational level, transferable in time and space

PARAMETERS FOR SUCCESS

Typical mistakes with regard to Knowledge Management are usually situated in the human or organisational area. Have these been sufficiently addressed?

Therefore, success criteria are bound to be found in other than technical domains:

- ▷ Vision, strategy, goals
- ▷ Knowledge worker central
- ▷ Time and priority
- ▷ Management (example and communication)
- ▷ Personal advantages
- ▷ Phased approach
- ▷ Change, maturity, culture, need
- ▷ Knowledge-oriented function description

Vision, strategy, goals

Answering information and knowledge needs is not about ICT. You need a vision and strategy partner to help you discover your setting and values.

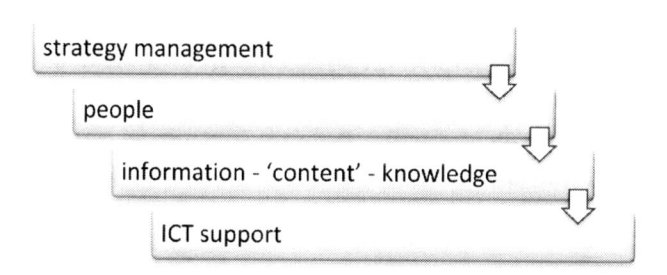

```
strategy management
    ⇓
  people
    ⇓
  information - 'content' - knowledge
    ⇓
  ICT support
```

As long as an organisation, or its management, is not aware of the information pain in the organisation, not a lot will happen.

Central position of the knowledge worker

As managers, we mainly work with people. The organisation and its culture are formed by people. The same people are the ultimate source and the users of information and knowledge in the organisation.

For reasons of efficiency and productivity, as well as competitive advantage, people must play a more central role and should be guided and supported as much as possible. People also hold on to habits. As every improvement means a change, it requires good communication and a broad basis. Don't expect all employees to be or become wildly enthusiastic straightaway. In every organisation, there are innovators, early adopters, late adopters and laggards.

Time and priority

Especially in a start-up phase, employees must be allowed time for the creation, maintenance and enrichment of quality information. Employees cannot record and share their information and knowledge with their colleagues if they are not allowed the necessary time to do so.

For instance, time should be foreseen for briefly recording experience gained after a project, recording new rules and making them accessible, making expertise traceable (who knows what), etc.

After the start-up phase, the creation and maintenance of information and knowledge will be more ingrained in the users' processes and tasks, and will require less effort.

Management (example and communication)

As an organisation, you need someone in charge of knowledge and information to direct the whole project as leader and pioneer. This person not only leads the implementation, but also keeps the wheel turning afterwards, makes sure that the knowledge and information problem receives continuous attention.

It is crucial that this person receives visible and real power from senior management to achieve all this.

A supporting steering committee should assist the person in charge of knowledge and information. After all, a correctly formed steering committee creates a cross-functional basis within the organisation.

The definition and communication of the shared meanings of taxonomies or – even better – contextual (TiNK®) properties, concepts and keywords within the organisation are extremely important and deserve due attention. In other words, make sure that everyone 'speaks the same language'.

Prove personal advantages

Employee support is an essential element in every implementation or (positive) change. It can be achieved through:

- ▷ Consensus about its necessity
- ▷ The fact that employees are the requesting party
- ▷ An inquiry round (people will feel involved)
- ▷ Dealing with 'their' problems
- ▷ 'A say' and involvement in the phasing of the solution
- ▷ 'A say' and involvement in the elaboration of the solution (people will recognise 'their' problems)

The foundation of all improvements — hence, changes — for the user is his or her personal benefit. When users do not see a direct or indirect personal benefit, they will not be inclined to contribute to change or put in an extra effort.

A system, a solution, is an instrument that helps users to reach their objectives (dealing with information and knowledge in an efficient and effective manner). A solution should be integrated into the employee's work environment and work processes as much as possible.

At the same time, an (IT) solution should be as simple and user-friendly as possible to avoid possible extra barriers for the users.

Phased approach

The next element is the willingness, the disposition, to start with information management. Too many organisations lull themselves to sleep when it comes to tackling fundamental issues.

For the implementation, a step-by-step approach is preferable. Generic information management requires neither a 'big bang' start-up nor a 'mushroom' approach (the phenomenon of several unstructured small initiatives aimed at individual problems with a limited solution). A continuous, orchestrated series of small-scale implementations is recommended, although not always feasible.

Knowledge-oriented function description

When management is convinced that knowledge, information and documents are an important ingredient and growth factor for the organisation, it is strongly recommended this be incorporated into personal and team targets.

This way, it can become an evaluation criterion during the (half-) yearly appraisal and employees can be tackled about it. However, try to avoid translating it into financial benefits. Instead, translate it into recognition and respect as an employee becomes an expert in a given domain.

An example of personal targets:

Level 1	Acquires only the knowledge received from the organisation and required for the function.
Level 2	Searches for suitable knowledge within the scope of the function at his own initiative and reflects upon it for himself.
Level 3	Searches for suitable knowledge that goes beyond the scope of the function at his/her own initiative, systematically records this knowledge so that it also becomes available for others.
Level 4	Builds relevant (internal and external) networks and gathers suitable knowledge tuned to the organisation's basic objectives. Thinks about systems for storing this knowledge, maintains it to process, anchor and increase his own and common knowledge. Stimulates others to expand their own knowledge level continuously.

PERSONAL EXPERIENCES AND REFLECTIONS

Identify your organisational knowledge domains, limited to two levels.

For each of the domains and subdomains:

▷ Indicate the status and opportunities
▷ Indicate the strategic importance

Identify potential lacking elements to be successful on Knowledge Management in your organisation.

How can you sabotage a Knowledge Management initiative?

Have a look on <u>www.knowliah.eu/kcm/5</u> for other questions, ideas, discussion and answers on this topic.

The Knowledge Management building blocks

Knowledge Management is not an isolated phenomenon, but the most important cornerstone of our knowledge economy, sustained entrepreneurship, intellectual challenges, good management and innovation.

KNOWLEDGE VALUE

A first quick assessment of the value of information and knowledge is determined by four or so parameters. Value is an important deciding parameter for your final prioritisation and focus on initiatives and knowledge domains.

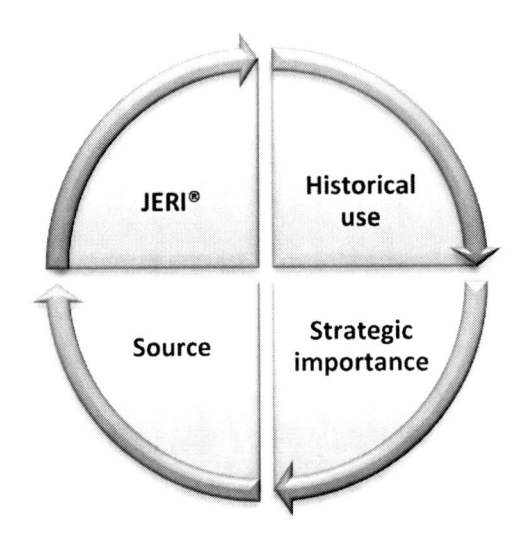

Circular diagram with four quadrants: JERI®, Historical use, Strategic importance, Source.

Historical use

80% of information is never used. Which 80%? And why would you invest time and energy in the creation, dissemination and maintenance of information that is not used by anyone?

Strategic importance

Even though a given domain is not used today, that does not mean it cannot become important sometime in the future. It is an important point of attention to translate an organisation's changing strategy and objectives continuously into a knowledge- and information-oriented interpretation.

The source

Not everyone is able to make an equally useful contribution to every domain.

▷ Who is the source of an information object?
▷ Who has validated this, on the basis of which expertise?
▷ Is the text maintained at regular intervals?

JERI®

Everyone is confronted with information stress, an abundance of documents and email. When you are confronted with an abundance of anything, you are no longer able to get down to what is really important as it gets lost in the large volume.

Therefore, it is crucial that you provide only the most relevant information to your employees and protect them from the sheer profusion of information and communication.

JERI® – Just Enough Relevant Information,
WHEN AND WHERE NEEDED

For the best results on the basis of your expertise, you yourself, your colleagues and your entire organisation need JERI®. No piles of information or terabytes on a server, but 'Just Enough Relevant Information', where and when needed.

JERI® means something different for each use. It is linked to:

- ▷ Context
- ▷ Responsibilities
- ▷ Interests
- ▷ Active (or missing) knowledge

CONTEXT AND MODEL

To be able to achieve JERI® for the knowledge worker, you need two elements:

- ▷ An information model on the basis of contextual enrichment (for instance, the TiNK® method)
- ▷ Set-up of the user's profile on the basis of this information model
    - ▷ in function of:
        - ▷ responsibilities
        - ▷ tasks
        - ▷ knowledge development
    - ▷ in function of interests

TiNK® method

Origin

The traditional approach of information and knowledge categorisation is the building of a fixed tree structure which serves as a basis for an improved dissemination of the available information. Recent variations are taxonomies, facet taxonomies and ontologies.

The main disadvantage of such an approach – the standard up until now – is that it always results in endless discussions and a long implementation course. Moreover, IT systems that are based on this approach do not seem to offer a solution to the information problem in practice.

Fixed structures do not work:

▷ Up to 50% of files are stored in the wrong location
▷ People, teams and departments have their own wishes with regard to the tree structure
▷ Certain information must be put in several locations
▷ Creation of 'trash' folders such as 'draft', 'temporary', etc.
▷ Users are unable to find their information in the current tree structures
▷ Uncertainty about which is the latest version as files have been placed in multiple tree structures: on the central server, locally on computers of various users, on department servers, in email systems, etc.

Because of the disadvantages of taxonomies, facet taxonomies and ontologies, we wanted to offer a practical alternative that meets the 80/20 rule: 80% effort spent on use vis-a-vis 20% effort spent on creation and maintenance.

As an alternative for unstructured information and knowledge, ICMS Group has developed the TiNK® method, which focuses on human cognition. TiNK® is an alternative that deals with information in a flexible and dynamic way and is based on contextual enrichment.

What is ...?

TiNK® is short for Transferring Information aNd Knowledge. More detailed information on this method can be found in the book *Learning to swim in information* by Hans Van Heghe or can be obtained from ICMS Group on simple request.

Research (conducted by ICMS Group in collaboration with the K.U.Leuven) and experience of experts in this domain have taught us that every human being executes a typical process with regard to information and knowledge.

TiNK® allows us to convert knowledge in people's heads into structured information by adding meta information and meta knowledge. As this is done during the normal work process, there is no need for a separate team of knowledge managers nor should the activity be restricted to a certain department.

In other words, knowledge is translated into a combination of the actual content of the information plus meta knowledge (cognition), plus meta information (context).

Categorisation of information is done according to the TiNK® method. Instead of placing the information in a fixed tree structure, we apply contextual enrichment using predefined input profiles called TiNK® skeletons. Thanks to these, consistency of storage and accessibility is guaranteed.

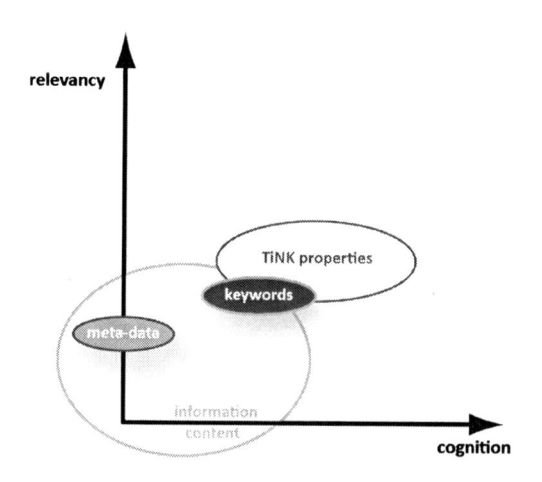

TiNK® Models

Origin

Based on our experience with TiNK® implementations and knowledge of your information flows and business processes, we have developed predefined information industry models. We also have a TiNK® industry Model available for your sector and/or functions.

TiNK® industry Models allow us to achieve:

▷ Faster and easier implementations of information management
▷ Integrated and consolidated information management
▷ Quick wins on information productivity
▷ Faster ROI
▷ More emphasis on the users
▷ More time and energy for your business opportunities

TiNK® industry Models are a true best-practice on information management for your sector and/or function which is information- and knowledge-sensitive.

TiNK® Models

A TiNK® industry Model is a set of pre-configured elements oriented towards your sector and/or function:

▷ TiNK® properties – context characteristics of your information
▷ TiNK® skeletons – search- and task-oriented sets of context characteristics for consistent storage and easy searching
▷ Dynamic Views – browsing your information from different angles

Your information/knowledge model

Your meta model for Knowledge Management contains different types of TiNK® properties (meta data):

▷ Properties representing your knowledge domain (limit your domain hierarchy to three levels)

▷ Properties indicating maintenance and approval processes (status, expiry date, appreciation by other experts etc.)

▷ Properties indicating security and target audience (see other remarks on security)

SUBJECTIVE PROFILES

A profile is more than a synopsis of a person's current position or responsibility.

TiNK®'s Expert Locator incorporates user-related information. This includes an expertise profile and an interest profile.

▷ Based on someone's *contribution* to information, TiNK® calculates an *actual* and dynamic expertise profile (to find the most relevant expert). This profile represents the competence domain(s) an expert is active in

▷ Based on *behaviour*, contribution and search queries performed, TiNK® keeps track of a dynamically changing *interest* profile (profile-based search result)

Business processes

Introduction

Daily tasks may or may not be carried out on the basis of business processes. But have the information and knowledge that are needed to carry out the process correctly been taken sufficiently into account in these processes? Which information and knowledge is created that can be useful for another knowledge player?

BPM

Since BPM – Business Process Management – is a widely known subject, we feel no need to elaborate on this.

Case Workflows

Case Management is a relatively new type of workflow implementation that was developed as a reaction to three *defects/disadvantages* that are often encountered with the use of *traditional workflow:*

▷ Analysis, modelling and configuration of processes often takes a lot of time and has a discouraging effect

▷ Traditional workflow routes 'work' in the form of individual activities and, as a result, users concerned do not have sufficient overview and information (context tunnelling)

▷ Starting or skipping extra activities or tasks during the execution of the workflow is not possible, hence these must be modelled in advance, which leads to complicated and complex processes

In Case Workflow, processes are modelled at a higher level and with much less detail compared to traditional workflow. The starting point here is not the internal flow with its multitude of tasks, but quality of service and communication with the customer. In other words, case workflow puts the focus on the case, or rather the case file, instead of on the task.

FLOOW method

FLOOW is short for Flexible Object-Oriented Workflow and uses the TiNK® method as a starting point.

The objectives of the FLOOW method are aimed at solving the disadvantages of the traditional BPM configurations. FLOOW simplifies workflows and gives them a contextual configuration. This way, the most important disadvantages (i.e. complex, too much time and energy needed, difficult to maintain) are solved in a pragmatic way.

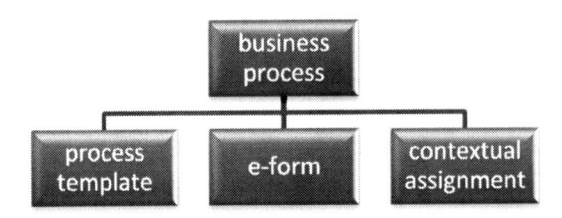

```
                    business
                    process
          ┌────────────┼────────────┐
      process       e-form      contextual
      template                  assignment
```

In addition to the traditional components (i.e. process engine and step-based e-form), the contextual assignment of processes and notifications is the single most important element.

This is a significant difference with huge advantages compared to traditional BPM flows.

p1	p2	p3	p4	WF	s1	s2	s3	s4	s5
v1	v1	v1	v1	wf a	r1	r2	r3		
v2	v2	v2	v2	wf b	r2	r3			
v3	v3	v3	v3	wf c	r4	r5	r6	r7	r8
v4	v4	v4	v4	wf c	r5	r6	r7	r8	r9
v5	v5	v5	v5	wf c	r6	r7	r8	r9	r10

On the basis of the context of a file/case/document/email, the appropriate process is selected and further defined/filled in.

FLOOW can be used for the traditional BPM and the more recent Case Workflow.

For more details on the FLOOW method, contact us at *info@icms.be* for a white paper on this subject.

Knowledge in business processes

Why

When defining and documenting important business processes, do you take care of the 'why' in the process? This 'why' is important for people involved in business processes. It prevents them from acting like a machine and brings in human involvement/touch.

- ▷ Why do I execute these tasks?
- ▷ Where do they fit in?
- ▷ Why are we doing this task this way?

How

'How' is the most evident reason for technical know-how.

- ▷ How do I need to execute those tasks in the most efficient and effective way?

Room for improvement

Knowledge-driven organisations motivate their people to continuously look for improvements, process optimisations, more effective ways to achieve the same goals and objectives.

A lot of the time, knowledge workers become frustrated by 'idea boxes' due to the lack of implementation and follow-up by management of their 'excellent' ideas. Will these people bring you another 'excellent' idea again?

Delivering new knowledge to the previous or next process step

The most benefit can be achieved by making people talk with others involved in previous and next steps in the business process. Understanding the how and why from each other is the basis for:

- ▷ Respecting each other's contributions
- ▷ Real innovation and optimisation in your business processes

COMMUNICATION AND WRITING

What is...?

Communication is the transfer of information between the location where the information originates and the point of receipt, without a change in form, content or order. Hence, the **communication process** consists of a sender (of the information), a message (the information) and a receiver (of the information).

Communication is usually a form of **two-way traffic:**

▷ Sending
▷ Receiving
▷ Feedback, or:
   ▷ interpretation ('translation' of the message)
   ▷ reaction (testing the interpretation against the original need)

Most organisations may be rich in information, but they are often poor in communication. And to make matters that little bit worse, the more important the news, the less it is talked about ('communicated').

In many cases, **communication problems** within an organisation have a tendency to grow even faster than the organisation itself. Even though we have 21st century **communication means** at our disposal, our way of thinking about communication often remains stuck in prehistoric times. Experience shows that employees in many organisations still rely on the 'grapevine' (or even worse, on 'gossip') and other vague sources for the bulk of their information.

Obviously, the problem is that effective communication is difficult, certainly in large organisations, and that chances of policy and other principles being wrongly interpreted are rather great.

Communication in an organisation is the consequence of the information need and is required to inform everyone involved and concerned about the objective and the consequences of the outlined policy. This way, the organisation hopes to avoid negative rumours and demotivation, and stimulate the willingness to change.

The complexity of the issues facing management today taxes an organisation's capacity for change. To be able to handle increasing external insecurity, organisations need to organise themselves differently, which often results in the usual internal insecurity. Communication, then, is mainly used to take away that (internal) insecurity.

To be able to communicate, at least two conditions must be met:

- ▷ Motivation (paying attention): people must want to send/receive
- ▷ Capacity (understanding): people must be able to send/receive

Communication in an organisation definitely has something to do with wanting to understand what someone else means, which implies willingness to cooperate; if not, you are preaching to deaf ears.

The communication process is influenced by the organisation's structure and culture, which themselves were (hopefully) influenced by the organisation's strategy (which itself was influenced by the environment in which the organisation operates).

Communication carries a number of potential risks:

- ▷ Conscious/unconscious deformation:
    - ▷ mental factors: a memory like a Gruyère cheese, having trouble in pinning something down, (not) reading between the lines
    - ▷ emotional factors: fear, frustration, prejudice, etc.
- ▷ Censorship
- ▷ Political areas of tension
- ▷ Untimeliness
- ▷ Misinterpretation

There are two types of communication in an organisation: internal communication (corporate philosophy, strategy and results, commercial information, product news, image, competition, etc.) and external communication (marketing and public relations).

Communication in an organisation is important because information is necessary to achieve objectives and control the business processes. For internal communication, an organisation will want to tailor content and format primarily to objectives resulting from strategy and to business processes. Useful instruments for this are: manuals, memos, staff announcements, newsletters, information sessions, working lunches, etc.

Needless to say, good internal communication also requires a good telecommunication system and a good data communication system.

Deliberate management of the communication processes results in a strong(er) organisation, great(er) added value and more productive employees. Here, the objective is not better communication as such, but better company results.

Terminology and usage of words

As people, we communicate with other people – directly or via information carriers. Every form of communication is based on words, terms. Every word has its own definition as well as its own context in which it is used.

Terminology management is an important factor in the optimisation of our communication, our exchange of knowledge and information. Consequently, terminology databases are vital in any organisation.

Standardising terminology and making it unambiguous results in clearer information and less risk of communication and interpretation errors.

When we analyse the documents available in an organisation, we usually come to the following conclusions:

- ▷ 10% to 40% of the content is about definitions
- ▷ 50% to 85% of the explanatory texts differ from the 'official' definition (if there is such a thing) in the organisation

Modular information

Every document has a structure. In this document structure, we can distinguish a number of blocks that try to communicate a certain message or a combination of messages.

These large blocks in a document may themselves be broken up into smaller structures. In these, you can identify small, independent objects of information.

An information object is an independent unit of information, usually not larger than one or more paragraphs. An information object has only one message.

The term 'information granularity' is often used in this context. Does a document equal one information object, or is a document a collection of information objects – for instance, a meeting report?

Next to categorisation and contextual enrichment, information modularity is the most important basic concept of the TiNK® method.

As a taste of what's in store, take a look at the example about meeting reports below.

Example — meeting reports

Traditional approach	Every meeting results in one report with an indication of the meeting date. Next, these documents are saved in a folder structure:

> Reports
>
> > Management
> >
> > > Report 4 January 2009

Problem	If you want to know which points of a topic were discussed and when and which decisions were made, you will have to read through many — if not all — meeting reports.
Modularity	This means that, per meeting, every topic is saved in a separate file.
TiNK® properties	To every file, three TiNK® properties are assigned:

- ▷ Topic
- ▷ Date (e.g. 4 January 2009)
- ▷ Type of meeting (e.g. management)

Result	Thanks to the TiNK® method, you get several possible angles for browsing the information on the basis of the context properties and the modular approach:

- ▷ According to date, then according to topic
- ▷ According to topic, then according to date
- ▷ Others, by placing the TiNK® properties in a certain order

Thanks to this structured TiNK® approach, you can deal with the information in a more efficient and effective way.

Writing

Regarding writing

Verba volant, scripta manent!

Spoken words fly away, writing remains. Or as the Dutch saying goes: *wie schrijft, die blijft* (those who write will last forever)! Despite this incentive, for most people it is still a struggle (rather than a pleasure) to convert words to sentences, and convert sentences to coherent text.

Writing is a form of purposeful critical thinking according to a (conscious) strategy in order to solve a certain problem. This we know. However, there is no such thing as a 'standard', let alone perfect, writing process. Ask 10 writers about their writing process, and you will probably end up with 10 different opinions.

Writing is more than simply translating thoughts into written language; it is a process that involves different factors. Writing is also the skill that helps to get this mental process going and structure it.

There are writers who know exactly what they are going to write in advance (the Mozart types); then there are writers who only gain some insight during the writing itself (the Beethoven types).

Phasing

Even though many roads lead to Rome, if we critically evaluate all those 'own thoughts', we can still more or less distinguish a thread.

It is a fact that the writing process takes place in a structured way (this is important to ensure that writing can be organised and learned), even though there is no law that defines the order of the various phases.

A tentative and pragmatic phasing of the writing process could look as follows:

Phase 1: thinking ('look before you leap')

- Determining the subject
- Determining the objective
- Determining the target audience

Phase 2: examining ('forewarned is forearmed')

- Analysing the subject
- Determining the main question

Phase 3: writing ('finally!')

- Creating an outline (structure)
- Writing
- Re-writing

Knowledge worker perspective

Too much information

Issues

The information and knowledge problem is growing every day. Its importance is self-evident but if not, make sure you visit www.icms.be. Current solutions do not provide an answer to the increasing demand of our knowledge-driven economy. Organisations continue to struggle with large volumes of information, managed in an unstructured way. This often results in a chaos that changes and evolves every day.

Search engines can provide an answer where current solutions can't, especially when it comes to challenges such as:

▷ Avoiding long, flat lists of results that do not provide an answer;
instead:
  ▷ presenting search results per subject
  ▷ allowing for text mining
  ▷ allowing for associations
  ▷ supporting direct actions
  ▷ grouping near-duplicates
▷ Avoiding taxonomies or ontologies as they:
  ▷ require too much manual work
  ▷ are always running after the facts
▷ Integration of the user's profile to obtain better results and distinguish:
  ▷ an interest profile
  ▷ an expert profile
▷ Minimal implementation effort
▷ Integration of translations and synonyms in the search result
▷ As 40% to 50% of searches result in NO answer, searching for expertise, not only for documents
▷ Searching through multiple sources, not only on local computers

A solution

A usable solution needs to support the user and deliver JERI® (Just Enough Relevant Information) in the following way:

Classic search features

Your search engine needs to contain, like most other known search engines, features such as: exact occurrence, Boolean search (AND, OR), 'Do you mean?', relevance percentage, new and incremental indexing, searching on files, display of the result context (snippets), etc.

Widening the question

Don't miss out on anything! The system applies a strategy of widening your question to be sure nothing is missed. Translations, synonyms and exception lists are commonly used mechanisms in TiNK® for widening your question.

Narrowing the answer

The system applies a strategy to deliver the most relevant information with just a few mouse clicks. We call this JERI® – Just Enough Relevant Information, when and where needed.

Algorithms such as the McKnow technology also take the user's profile into account.

Subject grouping

Subject grouping folders present your search results in tree structures, generated on the fly on the basis of both content and context. This helps a user to fine-tune his/her question and avoids scrolling down long lists of search results.

Text mining

Mechanisms in the interface help the user to drill down and find related information in a natural way.

Associations

Based on key terms in the starting document, the system identifies documents with similar content.

Meta-filtering

Databases contain fields. Enterprise content systems contain categories. Some systems – like TiNK® – contain auto-classification engines.

These fields, categories, attributes and meta data can be used to help a user to filter results easily.

Action basket

You found what you needed, and then? An action basket provides features that can be carried out on search results such as: local save, email, print, start or add to a workflow, etc.

Personal profile

Optional integration of expertise profiles and interest profiles prevents noise in your search results; profile integration helps to adjust a search result towards a personal relevancy match.

Not enough knowledge

Issues

40% to 42% of searches result in NO relevant answer. This can be due to:

- No information being present
- Not knowing what to search for
- Being incapable of understanding the answer
- Getting lost in the large volume of information

At the same time, you are confronted with a huge pile of 'relevant' stuff to read, study, know. Our world, technology, procedures, legislation are growing every day. And you need to know it all!

A solution

Expert Locator

An Expert Locator incorporates user-related information. This includes an expertise profile and an interest profile.

Based on someone's **contribution** to information, the system calculates an actual and dynamic expertise profile (to find the most relevant expert). This profile represents the competence domain(s) in which an expert is active.

Based on **behaviour**, contribution and search queries performed, TiNK® keeps track of a dynamically changing interest profile (profile-based search result).

When a search result is insufficient or too complex to understand, an Expert Locator helps you to identify the most relevant expert(s) to:

- Explain the answers
- Give you additional better answers
- Create new knowledge validated by other relevant experts

Agents, knowledge watchers

Agents driven by context and personal profiles – i.e. knowledge watchers – facilitate the user in filtering the most relevant and applicable information and knowledge to know. No more brain indigestion.

As such, knowledge watchers can:

  ▷ Ensure that you are being informed
  ▷ Drive your learning initiatives

Learning on the job

Integrate in a user's work environment active notifications based on context and new relevant:

  ▷ Knowledge objects from other users
  ▷ Procedures, regulations and laws
  ▷ Developed domains

Relevant new knowledge presented during work may look like disturbance. However, practical experience shows that users are much more open and receptive to new knowledge.

COMMUNITIES

In a decentralised economy, international communities of experts or communities of practices or communities of interest are a modern way of communicating and collaborating on specific topics and problems.

Personally, I'm of the opinion that those communities are not sufficiently focused on tangible results and answers. Communities tend to focus on discussions instead of the answers those discussions need to lead too.

In a community, you need to understand and accept the different roles that are played by the members of a specific community:

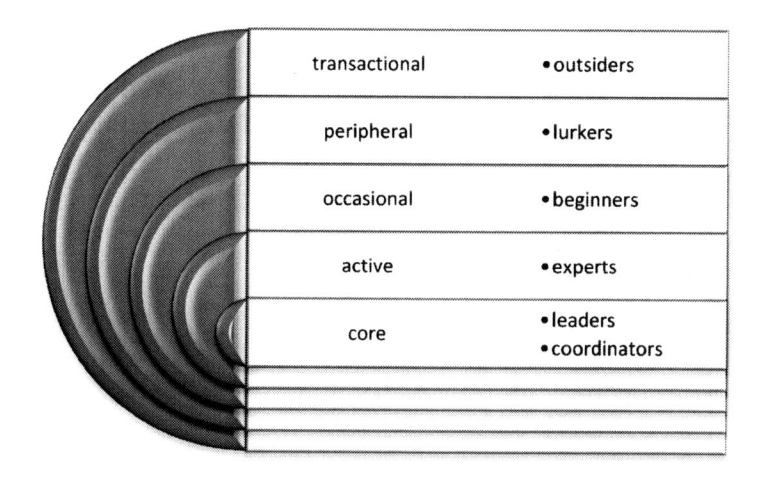

transactional	• outsiders
peripheral	• lurkers
occasional	• beginners
active	• experts
core	• leaders • coordinators

When you want to learn more on COPs, you should read the book *Communities of practice: learning, meaning, and identity* by *Etienne Wenger* from 1999.

Knowledge Management and learning

To improve your competences, you must learn or be trained. This is an important part of competence management. But the numbers are alarming: on average, learning in an organisation can be divided as follows:

▷ On-the-job learning 50%
▷ Learning by example (mentorship, coaching) 30%
▷ Training, formal courses 20%

In Europe, training and formal courses receive less than 10% of the attention (i.e. time and budget). The other forms are barely addressed or not at all.

In a learning organisation, the focus lies on the training aspect in combination with – in a number of cases – learning from experience.

The content, the internal knowledge is forgotten. Many e-learning projects fail because of a lack of own written-down knowledge that can be used for these trainings. Too much attention goes to the packaging or to trainings delivered by third parties.

Meta-filtering

Databases contain fields. Enterprise content systems contain categories. Some systems – like TiNK® – contain auto-classification engines.

These fields, categories, attributes and meta data can be used to help a user to filter results easily.

Action basket

You found what you needed, and then? An action basket provides features that can be carried out on search results such as: local save, email, print, start or add to a workflow, etc.

Personal profile

Optional integration of expertise profiles and interest profiles prevents noise in your search results; profile integration helps to adjust a search result towards a personal relevancy match.

A solution

A usable solution needs to support the user and deliver JERI® (Just Enough Relevant Information) in the following way:

Classic search features

Your search engine needs to contain, like most other known search engines, features such as: exact occurrence, Boolean search (AND, OR), 'Do you mean?', relevance percentage, new and incremental indexing, searching on files, display of the result context (snippets), etc.

Widening the question

Don't miss out on anything! The system applies a strategy of widening your question to be sure nothing is missed. Translations, synonyms and exception lists are commonly used mechanisms in TiNK® for widening your question.

Narrowing the answer

The system applies a strategy to deliver the most relevant information with just a few mouse clicks. We call this JERI® – Just Enough Relevant Information, when and where needed.

Algorithms such as the McKnow technology also take the user's profile into account.

Subject grouping

Subject grouping folders present your search results in tree structures, generated on the fly on the basis of both content and context. This helps a user to fine-tune his/her question and avoids scrolling down long lists of search results.

Text mining

Mechanisms in the interface help the user to drill down and find related information in a natural way.

Associations

Based on key terms in the starting document, the system identifies documents with similar content.

Too much information

Issues

The information and knowledge problem is growing every day. Its importance is self-evident but if not, make sure you visit _www.icms.be_. Current solutions do not provide an answer to the increasing demand of our knowledge-driven economy. Organisations continue to struggle with large volumes of information, managed in an unstructured way. This often results in a chaos that changes and evolves every day.

Search engines can provide an answer where current solutions can't, especially when it comes to challenges such as:

▷ Avoiding long, flat lists of results that do not provide an answer;
instead:
  ▷ presenting search results per subject
  ▷ allowing for text mining
  ▷ allowing for associations
  ▷ supporting direct actions
  ▷ grouping near-duplicates
▷ Avoiding taxonomies or ontologies as they:
  ▷ require too much manual work
  ▷ are always running after the facts
▷ Integration of the user's profile to obtain better results and distinguish:
  ▷ an interest profile
  ▷ an expert profile
▷ Minimal implementation effort
▷ Integration of translations and synonyms in the search result
▷ As 40% to 50% of searches result in NO answer, searching for expertise, not only for documents
▷ Searching through multiple sources, not only on local computers

Knowledge worker perspective

SECURING VERSUS SECURING

Securing as in securing your knowledge, capturing it, having it tested and validated is one definition of securing (see the section 'Lost knowledge').

Securing as in protecting, avoiding the so called 'knowledge leakage' is another definition of securing.

In a knowledge-centred organisation (see the section 'Evolution as a knowledge organisation'), knowledge is available to the entire organisation.

Depending on the nature, sensitivity, strategic importance and, of course, your internal culture and habits, it can be very wise to protect and restrict access to certain knowledge domains. See it as a proactive measure.

Next – or as an alternative – to protecting, you can also log and trace access and usage of key knowledge. Misuse is traced and reactive measures can be taken.

Thus, which approach is best suited for your organisation – reactive or proactive securing/protecting?

Personal experiences and reflections

Define for five functions/roles in your organisation their specific JERI® content domains.

Identify potential elements of your information/knowledge model applicable to your organisation.

Which elements of the writing process should be improved in your organisation?

> *Have a look on www.knowliah.eu/kcm/6 for other questions, ideas, discussion and answers on this topic.*

These large blocks in a document may themselves be broken up into smaller structures. In these, you can identify small, independent objects of information.

An information object is an independent unit of information, usually not larger than one or more paragraphs. An information object has only one message.

The term 'information granularity' is often used in this context. Does a document equal one information object, or is a document a collection of information objects – for instance, a meeting report?

Next to categorisation and contextual enrichment, information modularity is the most important basic concept of the TiNK® method.

As a taste of what's in store, take a look at the example about meeting reports below.

Example — meeting reports

Traditional approach	Every meeting results in one report with an indication of the meeting date. Next, these documents are saved in a folder structure:

    Reports

        Management

            Report 4 January 2009

Problem	If you want to know which points of a topic were discussed and when and which decisions were made, you will have to read through many — if not all — meeting reports.
Modularity	This means that, per meeting, every topic is saved in a separate file.
TINK® properties	To every file, three TiNK® properties are assigned: ▷ Topic ▷ Date (e.g. 4 January 2009) ▷ Type of meeting (e.g. management)
Result	Thanks to the TiNK® method, you get several possible angles for browsing the information on the basis of the context properties and the modular approach: ▷ According to date, then according to topic ▷ According to topic, then according to date ▷ Others, by placing the TiNK® properties in a certain order Thanks to this structured TiNK® approach, you can deal with the information in a more efficient and effective way.

Writing

Regarding writing

Verba volant, scripta manent!

Spoken words fly away, writing remains. Or as the Dutch saying goes: *wie schrijft, die blijft* (those who write will last forever)! Despite this incentive, for most people it is still a struggle (rather than a pleasure) to convert words to sentences, and convert sentences to coherent text.

Writing is a form of purposeful critical thinking according to a (conscious) strategy in order to solve a certain problem. This we know. However, there is no such thing as a 'standard', let alone perfect, writing process. Ask 10 writers about their writing process, and you will probably end up with 10 different opinions.

Writing is more than simply translating thoughts into written language; it is a process that involves different factors. Writing is also the skill that helps to get this mental process going and structure it.

There are writers who know exactly what they are going to write in advance (the Mozart types); then there are writers who only gain some insight during the writing itself (the Beethoven types).

Phasing

Even though many roads lead to Rome, if we critically evaluate all those 'own thoughts', we can still more or less distinguish a thread.

It is a fact that the writing process takes place in a structured way (this is important to ensure that writing can be organised and learned), even though there is no law that defines the order of the various phases.

A tentative and pragmatic phasing of the writing process could look as follows:

Phase 1: thinking ('look before you leap')

- ▷ Determining the subject
- ▷ Determining the objective
- ▷ Determining the target audience

Phase 2: examining ('forewarned is forearmed')

- ▷ Analysing the subject
- ▷ Determining the main question

Phase 3: writing ('finally!')

- ▷ Creating an outline (structure)
- ▷ Writing
- ▷ Re-writing

NOT ENOUGH KNOWLEDGE

Issues

40% to 42% of searches result in NO relevant answer. This can be due to:

- ▷ No information being present
- ▷ Not knowing what to search for
- ▷ Being incapable of understanding the answer
- ▷ Getting lost in the large volume of information

At the same time, you are confronted with a huge pile of 'relevant' stuff to read, study, know. Our world, technology, procedures, legislation are growing every day. And you need to know it all!

A solution

Expert Locator

An Expert Locator incorporates user-related information. This includes an expertise profile and an interest profile.

Based on someone's **contribution** to information, the system calculates an actual and dynamic expertise profile (to find the most relevant expert). This profile represents the competence domain(s) in which an expert is active.

Based on **behaviour**, contribution and search queries performed, TiNK® keeps track of a dynamically changing interest profile (profile-based search result).

When a search result is insufficient or too complex to understand, an Expert Locator helps you to identify the most relevant expert(s) to:

- ▷ Explain the answers
- ▷ Give you additional better answers
- ▷ Create new knowledge validated by other relevant experts

Agents, knowledge watchers

Agents driven by context and personal profiles – i.e. knowledge watchers – facilitate the user in filtering the most relevant and applicable information and knowledge to know. No more brain indigestion.

As such, knowledge watchers can:

▷ Ensure that you are being informed
▷ Drive your learning initiatives

Learning on the job

Integrate in a user's work environment active notifications based on context and new relevant:

▷ Knowledge objects from other users
▷ Procedures, regulations and laws
▷ Developed domains

Relevant new knowledge presented during work may look like disturbance. However, practical experience shows that users are much more open and receptive to new knowledge.

LOST KNOWLEDGE

Issues

A number of organisational and personal activities lead to the loss of knowledge:

- ▷ Reorganisations
- ▷ People retiring or leaving the company
- ▷ People moving to other departments
- ▷ People being on holiday or on sick leave
- ▷ Mergers and acquisitions
- ▷ Sabbatical leave

Gone is the colleague that would help me solve problems or clarify complex issues. As managers, we don't always have a clear and prompt answer to this.

A solution for lost knowledge requires a number of steps and is not achieved in a couple of months' time.

A solution

You can proactively build a knowledge base with validated and tested information covering your most important knowledge domains.

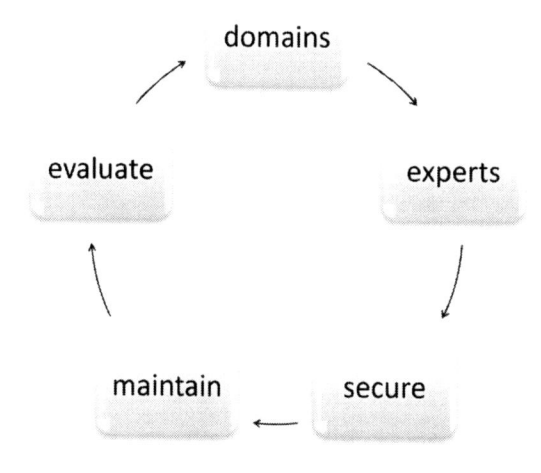

```
              domains
           ↗          ↘
    evaluate          experts
        ↑                ↓
    maintain  ←      secure
```

1 Identify crucial/important knowledge domains in your organisation

Identify, rank and position those domains with regard to:

- ▷ Business processes in the organisation
- ▷ Products, projects and services (incoming and outgoing flows)
- ▷ Target audience, hierarchy, departments and workgroups
- ▷ Other (technical) knowledge domains and sub-domains (limit to three levels)

Also identify the source of your knowledge domains. Not all of them are just coming from internal people; you also have external knowledge suppliers, knowledge from data (BI), etc. (see knowledge sources).

2 Identify key knowledge experts in each domain

For your internally sourced knowledge domains, you need to identify key knowledge experts in each domain and distinguish different levels (suitable to your organisation) such as:

- ▷ Coordinator
- ▷ Core contributors (leaders, active experts)
- ▷ Occasional contributors
- ▷ Beginners
- ▷ Outsiders

Be aware that this group and its roles are changing continuously and will require new contributors.

3 Define a knowledge securing procedure

Within each knowledge domain, you need to define your knowledge policy (with common elements for all knowledge domains):

- ▷ Internal prioritisation
- ▷ Available time for knowledge development
- ▷ Securing process and template (focus on core, avoid long prose)
- ▷ Validation and testing process

4 Define a knowledge validation and maintenance procedure

Information and knowledge become outdated (on average) within six to nine months. It is a key task to keep this validated information up-to-date.

5 Evaluate usage and importance

Social networks also allow you to request evaluation scoring from users. It is not a democracy, however. Depending on the objectives of your scoring, expert scoring might be more important, or reversed.

Next to usage, you also need to re-evaluate the strategic importance of all your domains as the world is changing quite fast.

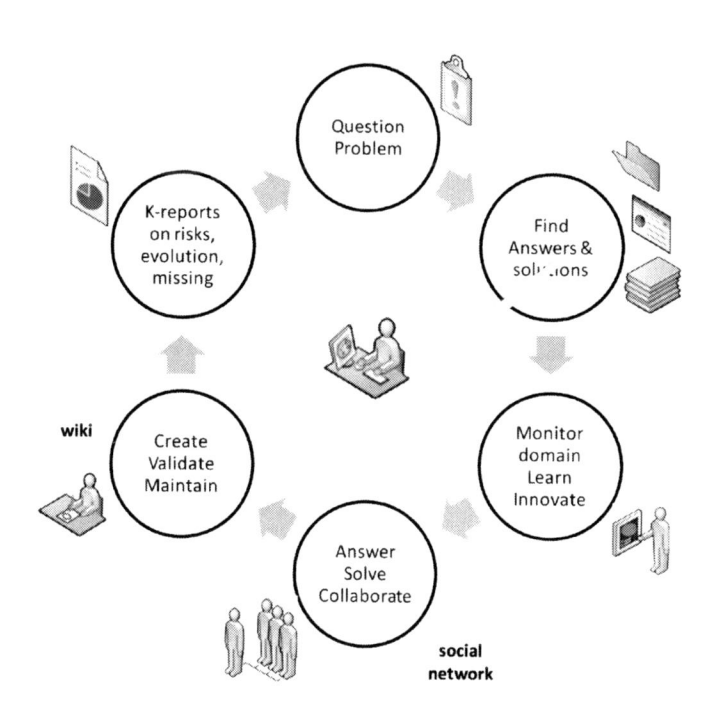

PERSONAL EXPERIENCES AND REFLECTIONS

List the top 10 most important (internal and external) information sources for your department.

For each of your top 10 strategic important organisational knowledge domains and subdomains:

▷ Indicate potential knowledge (retiring) risk
▷ Identify back-up people

> *Have a look on www.knowliah.eu/kcm/7 for other questions, ideas, discussion and answers on this topic.*

Knowledge organisation perspective

OPERATIONAL

In the operational domain, management is confronted with a series of questions to which knowledge centric management provides an answer:

- ▷ Are business processes carried out correctly and expertly?
- ▷ Are we sufficiently productive?
- ▷ Do we attain the right level of service?
- ▷ Do we use the right communication for the right target groups (internally and externally)?
- ▷ Can we avoid costs?

Productivity

Find faster

Results from international research and surveys indicate that we – as individuals – spend about *two to 13.5 hours* per week searching for information. Thanks to the unique TiNK® features in the federated search engine, the required time is reduced by over 50%.

Minimise re-invention

Fast availability of relevant information promotes re-use of reports, specifications, etc. Re-use has three levels: (1) direct copy, (2) copy and rework, rewrite parts of it, and (3) use it as background to improve your message and arguments.

Faster effectiveness of new hires

New people (new to the organisation or coming from another department) will find relevant information in their own way. Emails of their predecessors about relevant projects and customers will be available immediately.

Business processes

Faster problem-solving and innovation

Similar problems or relevant information will speed up issue-solving.

Availability of managed ideas, suggestions and demands will drive innovation in your organisation.

Reduced risks

Consolidated overviews and notifications when outstanding issues start having a risk profile will warn relevant people early and avoid extra risks.

Better decisions

Being better informed, being able to browse through consolidated information and communication from different angles, support from the most relevant expert – these TiNK® capabilities will help you, your management and knowledge workers to make better decisions.

Internal communication

JERI®, better informed

At the same time, you are confronted with a huge pile of 'relevant' stuff to read, study, know. Our world, technology, procedures, legislation are growing every day. And you need to know it all!

Agents driven by context and personal profiles – i.e. knowledge watchers – facilitate the user in filtering the most relevant and applicable information and knowledge to know. No more brain indigestion.

As such, knowledge watchers can:

- ▷ Ensure that you are being informed
- ▷ Drive your learning initiatives

Target audience

Different audiences require different messages: a different wording, an introduction, another level of detail, other phrasings, etc.

Usually, authors require extra training to shape their writing skills. Taking the target audience into account always receives due emphasis in such trainings.

Speed and service level

Current buzzwords – frequently heard – are putting more pressure on the knowledge worker:

- Time to market
- Time to make
- Return on investment
- Faster, better, etc.

The appearance of such terms in an organisation is an extra reason to deal with information and knowledge solutions in a proper way. The knowledge worker needs urgent support in order to survive the current information and business stress.

TACTICAL

In the tactical domain, management is also confronted with a series of questions to which knowledge centric management provides an answer:

- ▷ Do we know enough to make the right decisions?
- ▷ Do we know enough to assess potential risks correctly?
- ▷ What about our quality?
- ▷ How do the market and our competitors evolve?
- ▷ Do we meet regulations (compliance)?
- ▷ How do we deal with ideas and innovation?

Decision-making

Can you be sure to make the right decision:

- ▷ When not all relevant information is taken into account?
- ▷ When you are not able to review it from different angles?

In the decision-making process, we need more relevant quality background information in order to make well-considered decisions.

Risk management

Some organisations are already able to detect potential risks from numerical data by looking at the appearance of patterns.

The biggest potential for early-warning signals, however, is hidden in texts. Proper and complete risk management will require pattern detection from texts.

Innovation and ideas

Innovation as an idea box for your employees?

Innovation requires more than a box. Innovation is out-of-the-box thinking. Not just as an attitude of collaborators, but also a knowledge-supported activity.

The most productive innovation is re-using a solution or approach from a totally different domain. The following should be taken into account:

- ▷ How similar are they?
- ▷ How different are they?
- ▷ Who should you address?

Quality management

Most companies see quality management as a set of procedures. More mature organisations try to incorporate continuous improvements in their quality processes.

Good, but probably not good enough. The above approach leads again to information overload, too many procedures, too many different versions, etc., which leaves the co-worker with an uncertainty:

- ▷ Am I doing this correctly?
- ▷ Am I missing anything to comply with regulations or legislations?

Imagine activity-based notification of relevant procedures, legislation, rules, etc. How would this improve your quality management?

Compliance

Quite often, compliance is applied to figures, accounting, reporting. But compliance does not only apply to figures; it also applies to text and communication:

- ▷ Who was/is aware of what?
- ▷ Who needs to approve?
- ▷ Who needs to be informed?

Compliance is an extension of the same principles that apply to quality management. Just like quality management, it is about complying with regulations and the same issues of information overload, information stress, insufficient knowledge, etc. apply as well.

Market intelligence

Like private organisations, governments and non-profit organisations as well have to take care of market intelligence:

▷ What is going on?
▷ How can I better serve citizens or clients?
▷ What are other similar organisations doing?

Market intelligence is knowing what happens outside your organisation. And that is much more than the competition's sales figures, waiting for and using market studies, or taking a one-off look at websites and other public information.

STRATEGIC

And the tactical domain? Here too, management is confronted with a series of questions to which knowledge centric management provides an answer:

- ▷ What do we know?
- ▷ What don't we know?
- ▷ Which knowledge is used the most and is therefore needed?
- ▷ How does our knowledge evolve?
- ▷ Where are the knowledge risks?
- ▷ What do we need to know tomorrow?

Inventory of knowledge

'If only HP knew what HP knows' from Hewlett Packard in the 1980s is one of the most used quotes in the Knowledge Management area.

Management sure has an idea of what they know. However, in practice never correct, never complete, always the wrong volume or concentration. Even the best management without the proper Knowledge Management support will not be able to identify knowledge in its organisation.

Next to knowing which knowledge is present, it is even more important to know which knowledge is really used in our business and activities.

Do not confront your knowledge workers with a task such as 'making an inventory of our knowledge' – for multiple reasons:

- ▷ It will never be correct or complete
- ▷ It is immediately outdated
- ▷ The reason for doing so is hard to explain since it brings no direct and clear benefit to their environment
- ▷ They might even consider it as a threat

A good start – which is also immediately usable to your knowledge workers – encompasses the following three initiatives:

- Draw a three-level tree of your knowledge domains:
  Only two or three, not more (area – domain – sub-domain)

- For the organisation:
  Write out the core knowledge everybody in the organisation should know in each department
  Not more than two pages (in a normal font size)

- Per department:
  Write out the core knowledge everybody in that department should know in each specific department
  Not more than four pages (in a normal font size)

Now you have a correct basis for your introduction package for new employees and for internal trainings, and a correct frame (raster) for identifying important knowledge areas.

Nevertheless, elements that are still missing (such as usage of and interrelations between knowledge topics) need to be answered.

Evolution of knowledge

A next element in the strategic domain of knowledge centric management is the evolution of knowledge.

- How are knowledge topics used?
- How do new topics appear?
- How do existing topics become less used or disappear?

Knowing as management how your concentration, usage and volume of information and knowledge is shifting, changing, vaporising, appearing, etc. is crucial in your ability to master and value that knowledge.

Would you otherwise be able to:

▷ Place it in the right perspective or context?
▷ Respect its importance?
▷ Respect the knowledge worker/supplier?
▷ Apply its value to your business?

Evolution of knowledge is also a core element when it comes to managing knowledge risks in an organisation (see next).

Knowledge risks

When it comes to knowledge risks for all organisations, it results in two main domains:

▷ White spots or missing knowledge
▷ Black holes or domains that are weakly supported

White spots

Missing? Missing compared to what?

White spots can be identified when you compare your actual information and knowledge with two other elements:

▷ Based on your knowledge strategy (see next)
 Where you need to make an inventory of required knowledge and expertise in five, four, two and one years' time
 A delta analysis needs to be made in order to identify missing knowledge
▷ Based on your external world (sector, competition, similar organisations in other sectors, research results, etc.)
 A delta analysis needs to be made in order to identify missing knowledge

Your strategy and your external world are the reference for identifying missing knowledge in your organisation. And you need both! Your 'strategy' for the specifics of your organisation; the 'external world' as a monitor of the potentials that you missed for your sector.

Identified white spots do not oblige you to fill them. It is a valuable decision to not react on it as long as you are able to make that decision in the first place. Today, it is an unknown decision, since you don't know.

Black holes

Weakly supported?

Black holes are knowledge topics with two characteristics:

- ▷ Often used or strategic, and thus valuable to your organisation
- ▷ Only covered by one to three experts (depending on the total number of experts) in your organisation

Domains that are not valuable or that are covered by 10 or more experts are not a risk to the organisation.

Identification of black holes helps you to prioritise your knowledge securing initiatives. In practice, black holes reduce your volume of knowledge 'to be secured' by 60% to 90%.

While there is no obligation to react on white spots, black spots do have to be dealt with. As a knowledge centric manager, you cannot continue to operate with such risks.

Knowledge strategy

Knowledge on the above elements helps you to become a knowledge-centred organisation by applying knowledge centric management.

As such, it will help you to define your knowledge strategy in alignment with your organisational strategy, just like you do for other assets and production elements.

A knowledge strategy means that you know:

- ▷ What your knowledge is
- ▷ How it evolves
- ▷ What your risks are

Next, you need to translate this into initiatives and emphasise, respect and steer the development of knowledge in the right areas and domains.

At the same time, comparing your knowledge evolution with your knowledge strategy will deliver the required elements to measure your progress with regard to your knowledge objectives.

PERSONAL EXPERIENCES AND REFLECTIONS

Rank the different elements from the 'Knowledge organisation perspective' following the perceived (or requested) importance in your organisation.

Have a look on <u>www.knowliah.eu/kcm/8</u> for other questions, ideas, discussion and answers on this topic.

PART III

RESULTS OF GROWING KNOWLEDGE CENTRIC MANAGEMENT

This section deals with the results of Knowledge centric management.

How you can grow as an organisation:

- ▷ How to measure your current status
- ▷ How to measure your knowledge evolution
- ▷ How to value and calculate returns

Goal and objective of Knowledge Management

BECOMING KNOWLEDGE-DRIVEN

Today, we see a shift from an operationally-driven economy towards a knowledge- and information-driven economy. You might be distracted by environmental and financial issues in today's economy, but that does not change the fact that our economy is becoming increasingly driven by knowledge and information.

In this knowledge- and information-driven economy, organisations need to define their goal and objectives: defining which level of a knowledge organisation they need or want to attain.

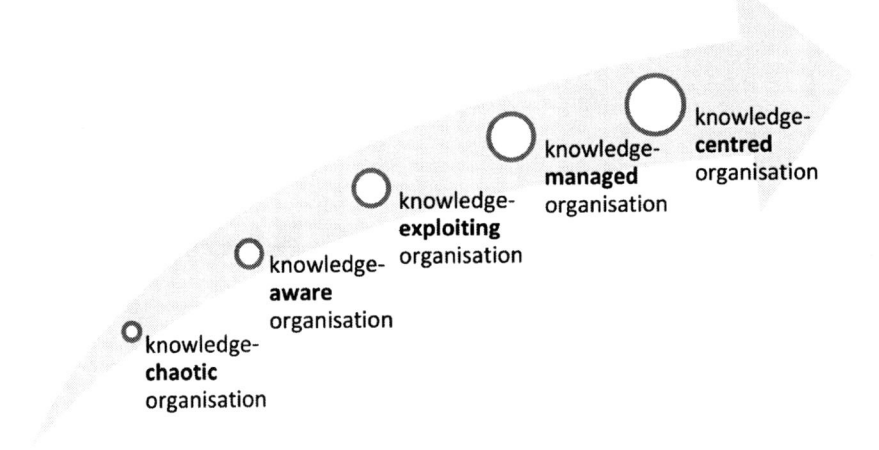

- knowledge-**chaotic** organisation
- knowledge-**aware** organisation
- knowledge-**exploiting** organisation
- knowledge-**managed** organisation
- knowledge-**centred** organisation

[see also Tissen, 2000]

Knowledge centric management

'Knowledge Centric Management' is the title of this book.

After 12 years of double occupation on information and knowledge, I do not believe Knowledge Management is the *nec plus ultra*.

Knowledge centric management is the objective we need to achieve, and Knowledge Management is the path towards it.

Defining Knowledge Management as an activity, as an occupation, with a dedicated manager, carries a number of risks.

First of all – and we have already encountered this in a number of organisations – it gives the other directors, managers, etc. an excuse for not participating in or contributing to Knowledge Management as it is the responsibility of the Knowledge Manager.

This behaviour will lead to another risk: a difference in word and deed. To quote Confucius:

> *"I don't understand what you say, because what you say and what you do is different."*

Knowledge Management is not an extra activity or task for you and your co-workers. It is only a consequence of our shifting western economy which is changing from a transactional economy towards a knowledge economy, where information, innovation and expertise are making the difference between more or less successful.

Knowledge centric management is a new type of management behaviour; it is a slightly different way of managing an organisation, a type of management where knowledge contribution as well as its optimal (re-)use and application is respected and valorised in business results.

PROMOTE RE-USE!

Instead of sending out the message to share knowledge, management should promote the *re-use* of each other's valuable information and knowledge.

In practice, it is the lack of re-use (and related respect) that limits the results of Knowledge Management, not the willingness to share knowledge.

Re-use is not just making a copy; re-use encompasses different levels:

- Direct
  the information or knowledge object is directly re-usable for your context
- Indirect
  the information or knowledge object needs reworking before being re-usable for your context
- Background
  the information or knowledge object provides relevant background information or earlier experiences for your case

As such, promoting re-use leads to an offensive approach (instead of a defensive approach with an emphasis on sharing) and leads to positive effects:

- Avoids re-inventing the wheel
- Improves productivity

PERSONAL EXPERIENCES AND REFLECTIONS

List your objectives and goals on Knowledge Management:

▷ Year 1
▷ Year 2
▷ Year 3
▷ Year 5
▷ Year 7

Have a look on www.knowliah.eu/kcm/9 for other questions, ideas, discussion and answers on this topic.

Growing versus Maturity

EVOLUTION AS A KNOWLEDGE ORGANISATION
Adapted Capability Maturity Model

The CMM consists of five levels. According to the SEI:

'Predictability, effectiveness and control of an organisation's processes are believed to improve as the organisation moves up these five levels. While not rigorous, the empirical evidence to date supports this belief.'

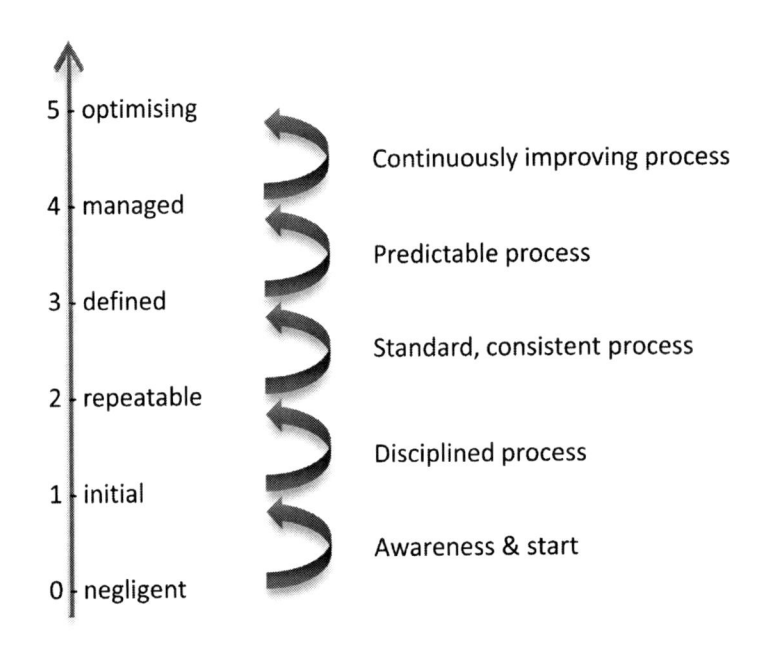

```
5 - optimising
                    Continuously improving process
4 - managed
                    Predictable process
3 - defined
                    Standard, consistent process
2 - repeatable
                    Disciplined process
1 - initial
                    Awareness & start
0 - negligent
```

Level 1 - Initial

At maturity level 1, processes are usually ad-hoc and the organisation usually does not provide a stable environment. Success in these organisations depends on the competence and heroics of the people in the organisation and not on the use of proven processes. In spite of this ad-hoc, chaotic environment, maturity level 1 organisations often produce products and services that work; however, they frequently exceed the budget and schedule of their projects.

Maturity level 1 organisations are characterised by a tendency to over-commit, to abandon processes in the time of crisis, and to not be able to repeat their past successes.

Level 2 - Repeatable

At maturity level 2, successes are repeatable.

Process discipline helps to ensure that existing practices are retained during times of stress. When these practices are in place, projects are carried out and managed according to their documented plans.

The status and delivery of services are visible to management at defined points (for example, at major milestones and at the completion of major tasks).

Level 3 - Defined

At maturity level 3, processes are well characterised and understood, and are described in standards, procedures, tools and methods.

The organisation's set of standard processes, which is the basis for level 3, is established and improved over time. These standard processes are used to establish consistency across the organisation.

A critical distinction between level 2 and level 3 is the scope of standards, process descriptions and procedures. At level 2, the standards, process descriptions and procedures may be quite different in each specific instance of the process (for example, on a particular project). At level 3, the standards, process descriptions and procedures for a project are tailored from the organisation's set of standard processes to suit a particular project or organisational unit.

Level 4 - Managed

Using precise measurements, management can effectively control the information and communication flows. In particular, management can identify ways to adjust and adapt the process.

A critical distinction between maturity level 3 and maturity level 4 is the predictability of process performance. At maturity level 4, the performance of processes is controlled using statistical and other quantitative techniques, and is quantitatively predictable. At maturity level 3, processes are only qualitatively predictable.

Level 5 - Optimising

Maturity level 5 focuses on continually improving information/knowledge performance through both incremental and innovative improvements. Quantitative improvement objectives for the organisation are established, continually revised to reflect changing business objectives, and used as criteria in managing process improvement.

Optimising information/knowledge that is agile and innovative depends on the participation of an empowered workforce aligned with the business values and objectives of the organisation. The organisation's ability to respond rapidly to changes and opportunities is enhanced by finding ways to accelerate and share learning.

A critical distinction between maturity level 4 and maturity level 5 is the type of variation addressed. At maturity level 4, information/knowledge is concerned with addressing special causes of variation and providing statistical predictability of the results.

At maturity level 5, information/knowledge is concerned with addressing common causes of variation and changing the process to improve performance (while maintaining statistical probability) to achieve the established quantitative improvement objectives.

Extensions

Recent versions of the CMM from SEI indicate a 'level 0', characterised as 'Incomplete'. Many observers leave this level out as redundant or unimportant, but Pressman and others make note of it.

Anthony Finkelstein extrapolated that negative levels are necessary to represent environments that are not only indifferent, but actively counterproductive, and this was refined by Tom Schorsch as the Capability Immaturity Model:

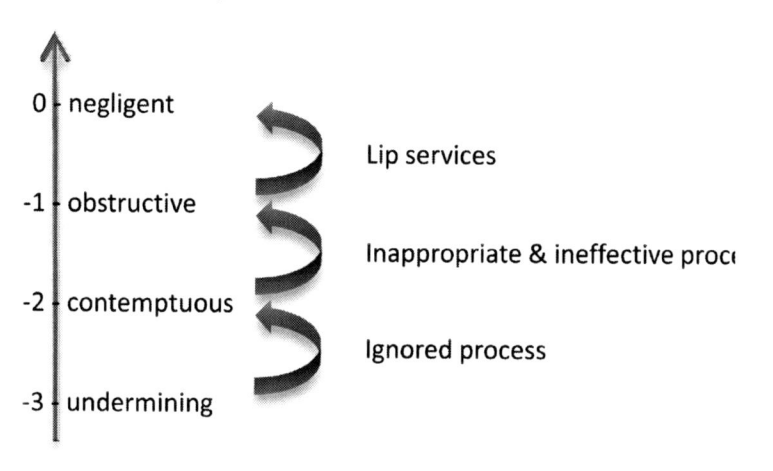

```
 0 — negligent
                          Lip services
-1 — obstructive
                          Inappropriate & ineffective proce[ss]
-2 — contemptuous
                          Ignored process
-3 — undermining
```

0: Negligent

The organisation pays lip service, often with excessive fanfare, to implementing software engineering processes, but lacks the will to carry through the necessary effort. Whereas CMM level 1 assumes eventual success in producing software, CIMM level 0 organisations generally fail to produce any product, or do so by abandoning regular procedures in favour of crash programmes.

-1: Obstructive

Processes, however inappropriate and ineffective, are implemented with rigour and tend to obstruct work. Adherence to process is the measure of success in a level -1 organisation. Any actual creation of viable product is incidental. The quality of any product is not assessed, presumably on the assumption that if the proper process was followed, high quality is guaranteed.

Paradoxically, level -1 organisations believe fervently in following defined procedures, but lacking the will to measure the effectiveness of the procedures they rarely succeed at their basic task of creating software.

-2: Contemptuous

While processes exist, they are routinely ignored by engineering staff, and those charged with overseeing the processes are regarded with hostility. Measurements are fudged to make the organisation look good.

-3: Undermining

Not content with faking their own performance, undermining organisations routinely work to downplay and sabotage the efforts of rival organisations, especially those successfully implementing processes common to CMM level 2 and higher. This is worst where company policy causes departments to compete for scarce resources, which are allocated to the loudest advocates.

GROWTH PROCESS

In a nutshell, the following phases can be distinguished in the knowledge awareness of an organisation

[combining 'CMM for Knowledge Management' by ICMS and 'The knowledge dividend' by Tissen, 2000]:

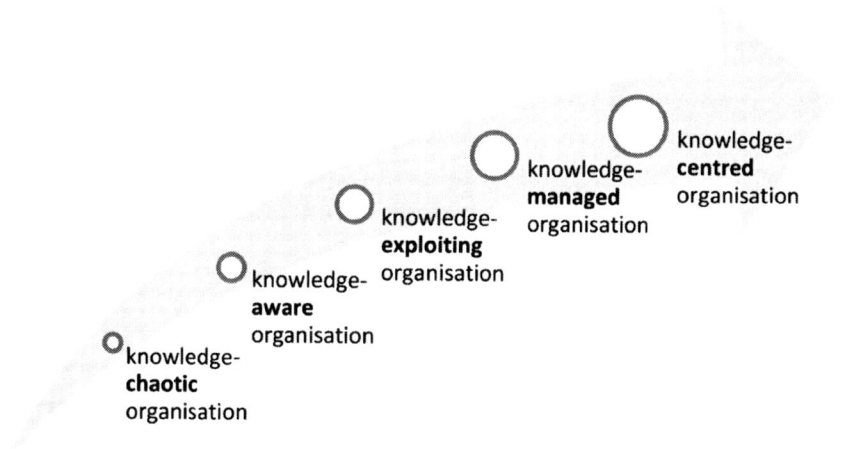

- knowledge-**chaotic** organisation
- knowledge-**aware** organisation
- knowledge-**exploiting** organisation
- knowledge-**managed** organisation
- knowledge-**centred** organisation

The knowledge-chaotic enterprise

The organisation is not aware of the importance of knowledge for meeting its strategic objectives. Data storage and management in the organisation takes place in an ad-hoc fashion. Access to information is difficult and time-consuming because the sources of knowledge are difficult to identify. The processes for retrieving information are inefficient or non-existent. There is no stimulation for making people save or share information.

The knowledge-aware enterprise

Knowledge processes and knowledge sources have been identified and documented. The retrieval of information has been simplified by the arrival of knowledge source catalogues. The implementation, however, does not encompass the entire organisation. Therefore, not everyone is up-to-date with regard to these knowledge structures. Ownership of knowledge and knowledge sharing are important issues.

The knowledge-exploiting enterprise

Knowledge Management already has a positive effect on turnover. Standard procedures and means (tools) are used in the organisation to regulate access to information memories. Knowledge bases (knowledge stores) are listed, evaluated and classified. The procedures for keeping these catalogues consistent have been implemented. A number of technological and cultural barriers are still to be overcome.

The knowledge-managed enterprise

The organisation has an integrated framework of procedures and tools for discovering, creating, maintaining and retrieving knowledge. The technological and cultural barriers have been overcome. The knowledge strategy is continuously adjusted and improved.

The knowledge-centred enterprise

The mission of the enterprise is the use and improvement of its knowledge base. This knowledge base provides a competitive advantage to the organisation. Knowledge is 'mission-critical' for the organisation.

PERSONAL EXPERIENCES AND REFLECTIONS

How far is your organisation on the 'knowledge driven' path?

Explain why and prove with examples.

> *Have a look on <u>www.knowliah.eu/kcm/10</u> for other questions, ideas, discussion and answers on this topic.*

Roll-out of Knowledge Management

PREPARATORY STEPS

Developing knowledge on Knowledge Management

Reading this book (and others of course) is already a first step towards acquiring knowledge on knowledge.

External experts can help you to develop more knowledge and learn more about this topic.

To assist organisations in this learning process, we have developed a number of workshops that can be considered as the minimum agenda to be covered by your external Knowledge Management coach:

- ▷ Introduction to Knowledge Management, a business perspective:
    - ▷ Knowledge about knowledge
    - ▷ Negative symptoms and impact of the knowledge economy
    - ▷ Importance of knowledge
    - ▷ What is Knowledge Management?
    - ▷ A framework for Knowledge Management
    - ▷ Conditions before starting
    - ▷ Actual status and objectives
    - ▷ Returns of Knowledge Management
- ▷ Implementing Knowledge Management in your organisation
    - ▷ Approach and tactics
    - ▷ Knowledge Management objectives linked to strategy
    - ▷ Knowledge Management processes
    - ▷ Tools and instruments (search, knowledge base, communities)
    - ▷ Prioritisation
    - ▷ Roadmap and implementation plan
    - ▷ Change and strong influencing elements

Communicate on Knowledge Management

Repeating clear messages to the end-user:

- What
    - what we are going to do
    - who is going to do this
    - when
    - for whom
- Why
    - personal benefit
    - managing expectations
- How
    - continuous
    - management support

Collaboration

Collaboration often refers to an approach that brings about a change in culture as well as in attitude:

From	To
The individuals who store their information on their hard drive	Making their information available in shared knowledge bases
Who waste their time re-inventing the information on the basis of 'who knows what'	More productivity thanks to re-use of the already acquired and improvement of the existing
Neglecting to remember the lessons in the groups	Sharing of expertise within different groups and departments
	Sharing of the acquired lessons and experiences

A bell curve on motivation

People are different in many ways. Openness to change and motivation are two of those differences.

In each organisation you find groups of people reacting in different ways:

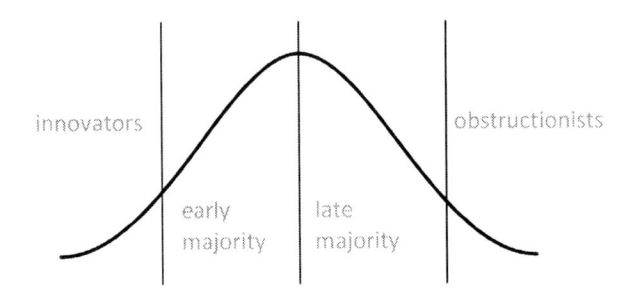

(bell curve diagram: innovators | early majority | late majority | obstructionists)

Each of those groups is responsive to other impulses:

▷ Innovators are convinced by clear arguments
▷ The early majority is convinced by one proven project (delivered by innovators)
▷ The late majority is convinced by 10 proven projects (delivered by early majority)
▷ Obstructionists can only be convinced by their individual personal benefits

A gain requires an investment

Each positive effect is initiated and achieved by an extra effort; 'no pain no gain' also applies to Knowledge Management.

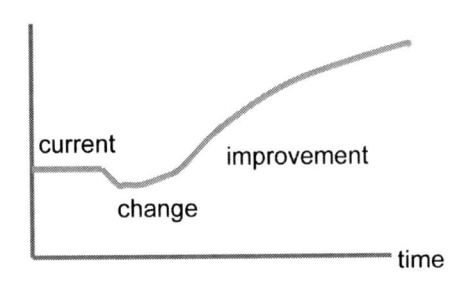

(diagram: current → change → improvement over time)

People change ... slowly

The following curve is well known to all of us.

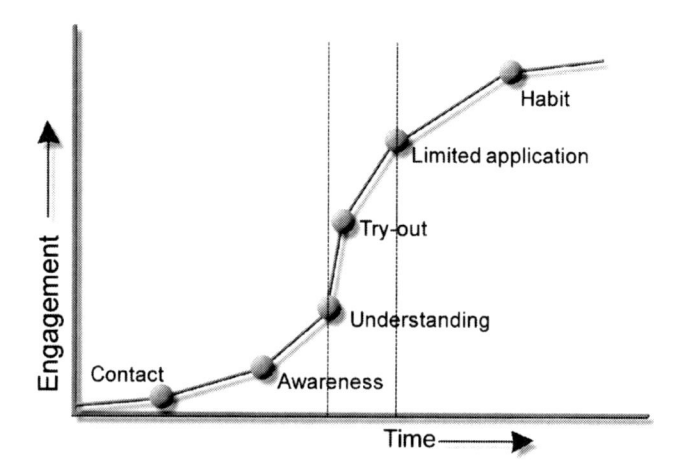

I want to draw your attention to the elapsed time between the two dotted lines. If this period is longer than two to three weeks, you will need to start your communication and motivation initiatives again. If people are not able to try out within maximum one week after understanding – and accepting – the message, they fall back to the previous state.

Personal experiences and reflections

Indicate your organisational readiness by scoring each of following elements (0: lacking completely – 5: fully implemented/available):

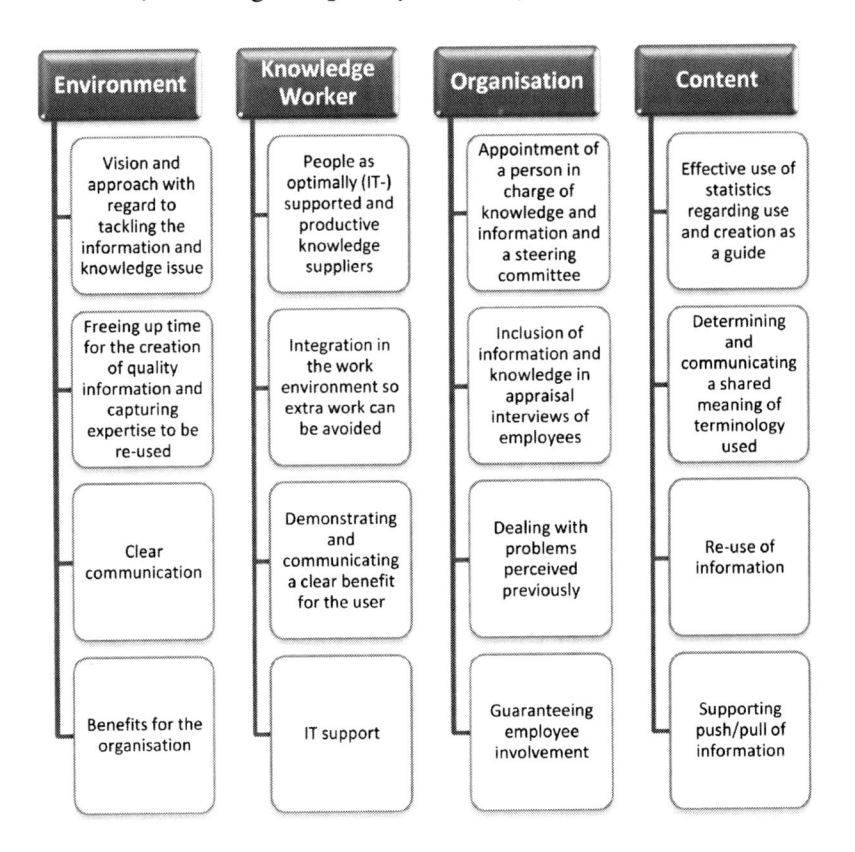

Environment	Knowledge Worker	Organisation	Content
Vision and approach with regard to tackling the information and knowledge issue	People as optimally (IT-) supported and productive knowledge suppliers	Appointment of a person in charge of knowledge and information and a steering committee	Effective use of statistics regarding use and creation as a guide
Freeing up time for the creation of quality information and capturing expertise to be re-used	Integration in the work environment so extra work can be avoided	Inclusion of information and knowledge in appraisal interviews of employees	Determining and communicating a shared meaning of terminology used
Clear communication	Demonstrating and communicating a clear benefit for the user	Dealing with problems perceived previously	Re-use of information
Benefits for the organisation	IT support	Guaranteeing employee involvement	Supporting push/pull of information

Have a look on www.knowliah.eu/kcm/11 for other questions, ideas, discussion and answers on this topic.

Defining your strategy and objectives for Knowledge Management

Today, we see a shift from an operationally-driven economy towards a knowledge- and information-driven economy. You might be distracted by environmental and financial issues in today's economy, but that does not change the fact that our economy is becoming increasingly driven by knowledge and information.

In this knowledge- and information-driven economy, organisations need to define their goal and objectives: defining which level of a knowledge organisation they need or want to attain.

A GROWING PROCESS

No 'big bang' approach

It goes without saying that Knowledge Management requires a phased approach, with small initiatives showing the potential of Knowledge Management, and allowing your organisation to learn about Knowledge Management:

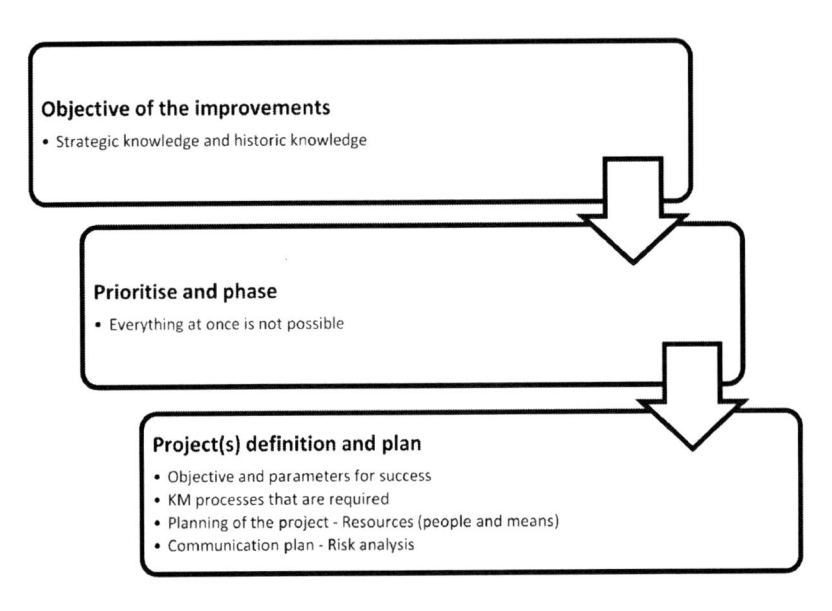

Objective of the improvements
- Strategic knowledge and historic knowledge

Prioritise and phase
- Everything at once is not possible

Project(s) definition and plan
- Objective and parameters for success
- KM processes that are required
- Planning of the project - Resources (people and means)
- Communication plan - Risk analysis

Project plan

Depending on your organisational project methodology (PMI, Prince2, etc.), the structure and content of your project plan might be completed differently.

However, make sure you cover the following crucial elements (see also Criteria for Success):

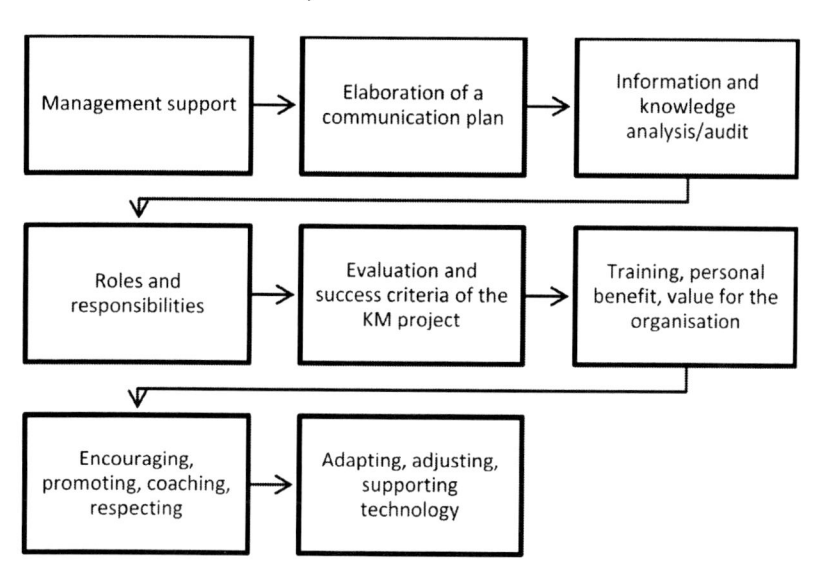

Management support → Elaboration of a communication plan → Information and knowledge analysis/audit

↓

Roles and responsibilities → Evaluation and success criteria of the KM project → Training, personal benefit, value for the organisation

↓

Encouraging, promoting, coaching, respecting → Adapting, adjusting, supporting technology

Evaluate your readiness

Before embarking on your different Knowledge Management initiatives, take some time to evaluate your tactics and roadmaps.

Evaluate the presence of the following elements in your project plan and in your organisation (all elements are mentioned earlier in this book):

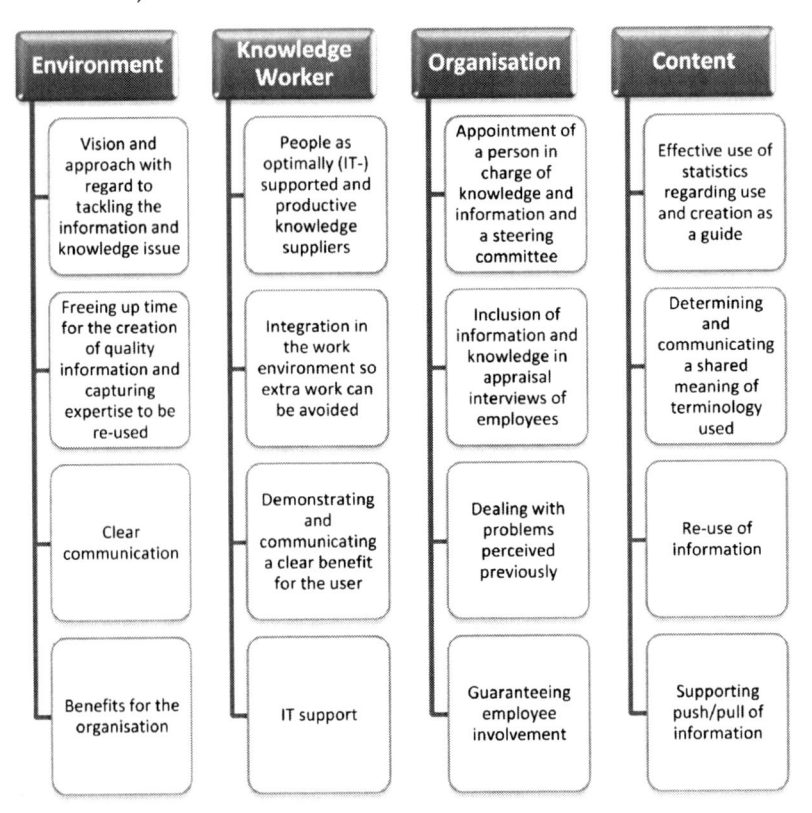

Environment	Knowledge Worker	Organisation	Content
Vision and approach with regard to tackling the information and knowledge issue	People as optimally (IT-) supported and productive knowledge suppliers	Appointment of a person in charge of knowledge and information and a steering committee	Effective use of statistics regarding use and creation as a guide
Freeing up time for the creation of quality information and capturing expertise to be re-used	Integration in the work environment so extra work can be avoided	Inclusion of information and knowledge in appraisal interviews of employees	Determining and communicating a shared meaning of terminology used
Clear communication	Demonstrating and communicating a clear benefit for the user	Dealing with problems perceived previously	Re-use of information
Benefits for the organisation	IT support	Guaranteeing employee involvement	Supporting push/pull of information

Implementing Knowledge Management

It is obvious: implementing Knowledge Management is quite different for each organisation. Nevertheless, a number of points of attention need to be respected and addressed.

Communicate on Knowledge Management

Repeating clear messages to the end-user:

- ▷ What
  - ▷ what we are going to do
  - ▷ who is going to do this
  - ▷ when
  - ▷ for whom
- ▷ Why
  - ▷ personal benefit
  - ▷ managing expectations
- ▷ How
  - ▷ continuous
  - ▷ management support

Collaboration

Collaboration often refers to an approach that brings about a change in culture as well as in attitude:

From	To
The individuals who store their information on their hard drive	Making their information available in shared knowledge bases
Who waste their time re-inventing the information on the basis of 'who knows what'	More productivity thanks to re-use of the already acquired and improvement of the existing
Neglecting to remember the lessons in the groups	Sharing of expertise within different groups and departments
	Sharing of the acquired lessons and experiences

A bell curve on motivation

People are different in many ways. Openness to change and motivation are two of those differences.

In each organisation you find groups of people reacting in different ways:

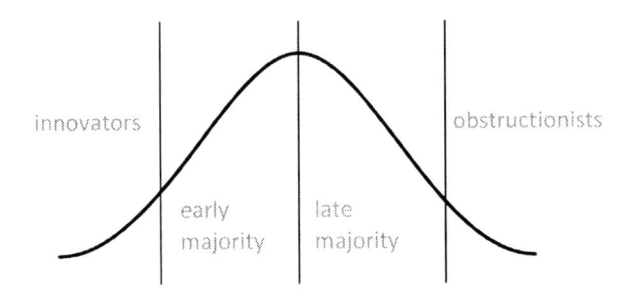

Each of those groups is responsive to other impulses:

▷ Innovators are convinced by clear arguments
▷ The early majority is convinced by one proven project (delivered by innovators)
▷ The late majority is convinced by 10 proven projects (delivered by early majority)
▷ Obstructionists can only be convinced by their individual personal benefits

A gain requires an investment

Each positive effect is initiated and achieved by an extra effort; 'no pain no gain' also applies to Knowledge Management.

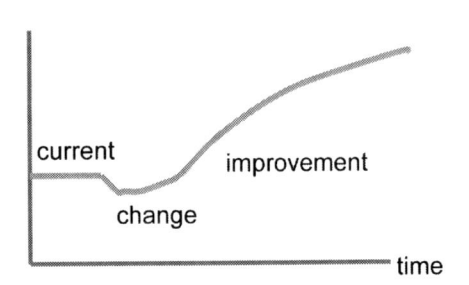

People change ... slowly

The following curve is well known to all of us.

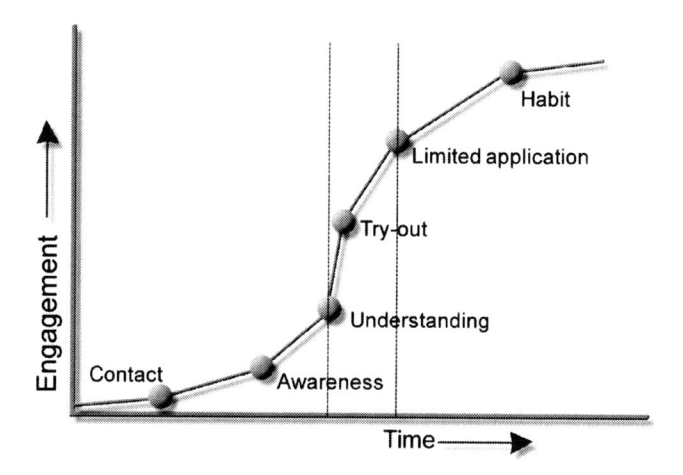

I want to draw your attention to the elapsed time between the two dotted lines. If this period is longer than two to three weeks, you will need to start your communication and motivation initiatives again. If people are not able to try out within maximum one week after understanding – and accepting – the message, they fall back to the previous state.

PERSONAL EXPERIENCES AND REFLECTIONS

Indicate your organisational readiness by scoring each of following elements (0: lacking completely – 5: fully implemented/available):

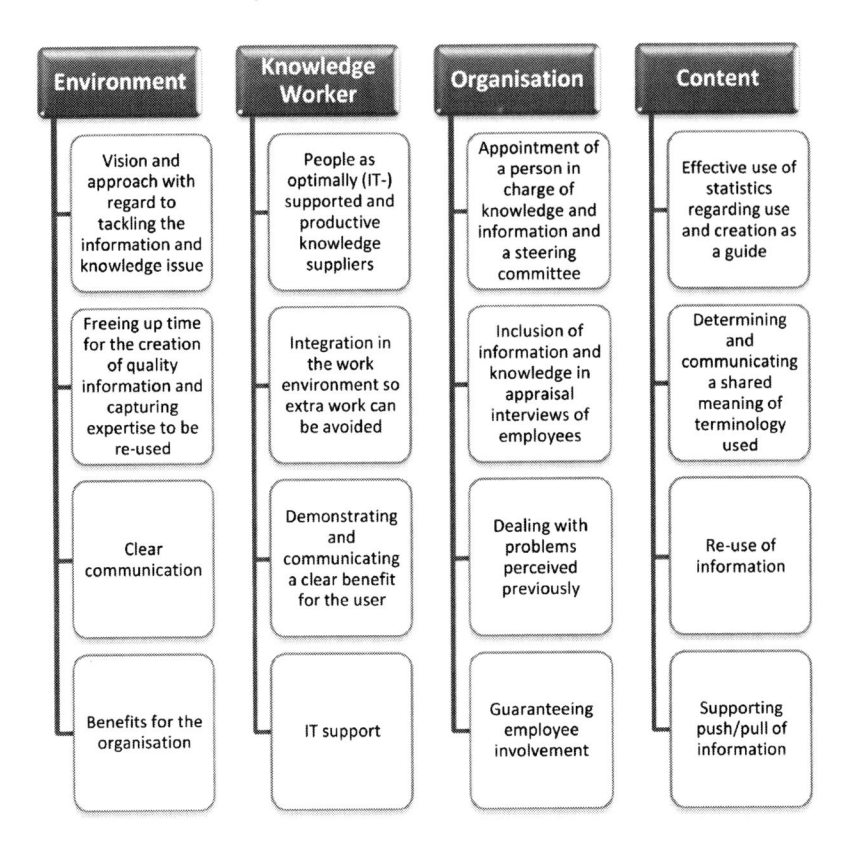

Environment
- Vision and approach with regard to tackling the information and knowledge issue
- Freeing up time for the creation of quality information and capturing expertise to be re-used
- Clear communication
- Benefits for the organisation

Knowledge Worker
- People as optimally (IT-) supported and productive knowledge suppliers
- Integration in the work environment so extra work can be avoided
- Demonstrating and communicating a clear benefit for the user
- IT support

Organisation
- Appointment of a person in charge of knowledge and information and a steering committee
- Inclusion of information and knowledge in appraisal interviews of employees
- Dealing with problems perceived previously
- Guaranteeing employee involvement

Content
- Effective use of statistics regarding use and creation as a guide
- Determining and communicating a shared meaning of terminology used
- Re-use of information
- Supporting push/pull of information

Have a look on www.knowliah.eu/kcm/11 for other questions, ideas, discussion and answers on this topic.

Measuring your evolution

AFTER THE IMPLEMENTATION

Knowledge Management does not stop after the implementation phase. Now the real work starts:

▷ Continuous coaching of knowledge workers
▷ Monitoring of usage (and potential leakage)
▷ Making sure experts and re-users are respected
▷ Ability to adapt to changing needs
▷ Etc.

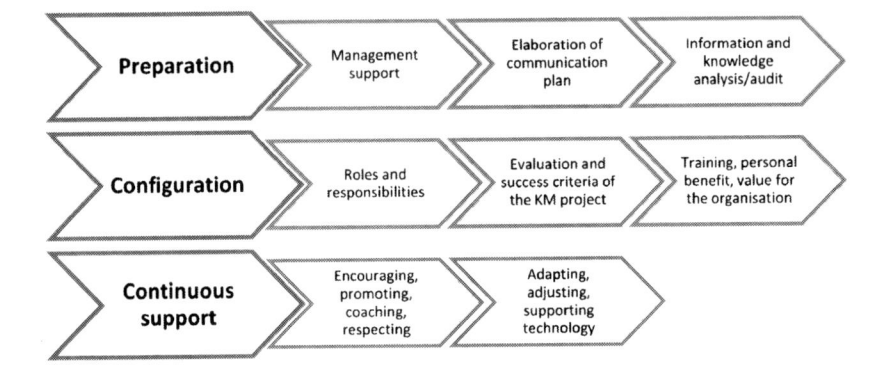

Preparation → Management support → Elaboration of communication plan → Information and knowledge analysis/audit

Configuration → Roles and responsibilities → Evaluation and success criteria of the KM project → Training, personal benefit, value for the organisation

Continuous support → Encouraging, promoting, coaching, respecting → Adapting, adjusting, supporting technology

24 ELEMENTS TO EVALUATE KNOWLEDGE MANAGEMENT, TODAY AND TOMORROW

Overview

You can evaluate your current status – and the progress achieved in the future – using the following 24 elements spread over five domains.

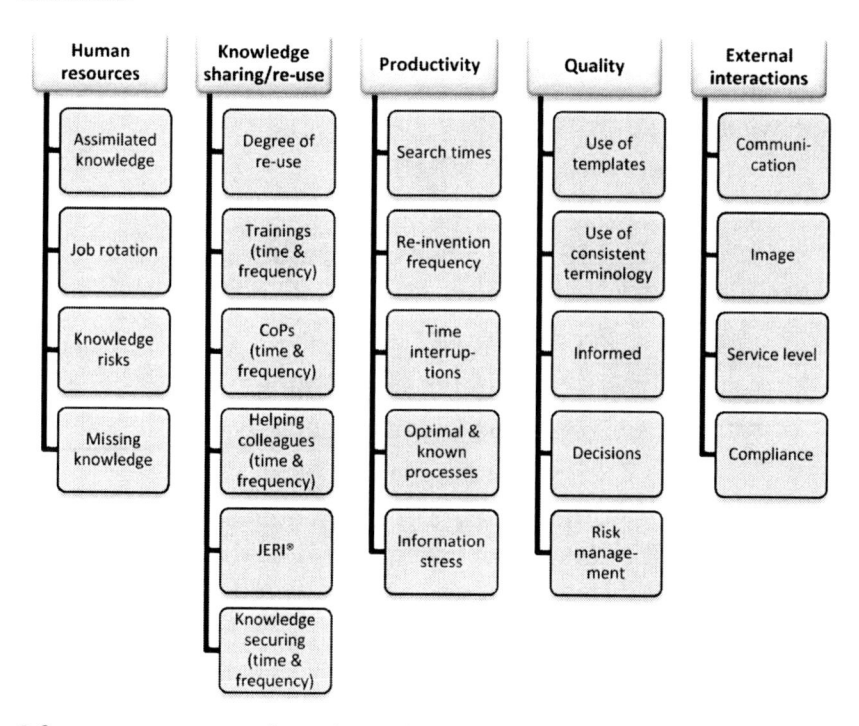

Human resources	Knowledge sharing/re-use	Productivity	Quality	External interactions
Assimilated knowledge	Degree of re-use	Search times	Use of templates	Communication
Job rotation	Trainings (time & frequency)	Re-invention frequency	Use of consistent terminology	Image
Knowledge risks	CoPs (time & frequency)	Time interruptions	Informed	Service level
Missing knowledge	Helping colleagues (time & frequency)	Optimal & known processes	Decisions	Compliance
	JERI®	Information stress	Risk management	
	Knowledge securing (time & frequency)			

Of course you can adapt this scheme to your organisational needs and emphasis. For example, pick the eight most important ones and focus on those eight, and add additional relevant elements.

CoPs: Communities of Practice

JERI®: Just Enough Relevant Information, when and where needed

Human resources

Evaluate and score your performance using the following indicators:

Element	Indicators
Assimilated knowledge	Per department ▷ Age and seniority ▷ Number of people ▷ <30 ▷ 30-50 ▷ 50-60 ▷ >60 ▷ Number of separate sites and offices
Job rotation	Per department ▷ Number of incoming /year ▷ Number of outgoing /year ▷ Number at risk /year
Knowledge risks	Who is expert in which domain? Number of experts per domain-region-section Degree of secured knowledge per domain-region-section
Missing knowledge	From actual operational perspective From strategic (future) perspective

Knowledge sharing/re-use

Evaluate and score your performance using the following indicators:

Element	Indicators
Degree of re-use	Time and frequency Part of tasks and job Easiness to find relevant knowledge Awareness on three levels of re-use Degree of 'not-invented-here' syndrome
Trainings	Time and frequency Number based on knowledge risks Number based on missing knowledge
CoPs	Time and frequency Number of CoPs per department Average number of collaborators (different types) Average amount of elapsed time CoP on line Degree of useful conclusion and closing
Helping colleagues	Time and frequency Percentage due to: ▷ Not understanding ▷ Not finding ▷ Not available ▷ Should know
JERI	Degree of viewing information my way Degree of profiled notification Number of context-driven processes Degree of automated classification Amount of used know-how
Knowledge securing	Time and frequency Part of tasks and job Type ▷ Domain-driven ▷ Question-driven ▷ Risk-driven Amount of know-how on the system Number of people contributing

Productivity

Evaluate and score your performance using the following indicators:

Element	Indicators
Search times	Frequency per day per type Time spent per query ▷ Searching ▷ Understanding answer ▷ Finding expert ▷ Interaction expert Degree of successful searches
Re-invention frequency	Frequency per day per type Time for: ▷ Solving problems ▷ Re-writing ▷ Re-answering
Time interruptions	Frequency per day per type Time for: ▷ Team ▷ Department ▷ Other Department
Optimal and known processes	Average number of processes Degree of optimisation Degree of access to required information within process Frequency of starting wrong process Frequency of escalations within processes Cycle times of processes
(Information) Stress	Number of terabytes of digital information and % used last year Library dimension and % used last year Number of subscribed periodicals Degree of: ▷ Too much information ▷ Missing knowledge Number of unread: ▷ Emails ▷ Documents ▷ Articles

Quality

Evaluate and score your performance using the following indicators:

Element	Indicators
Use of templates	Number of available templates Number of missing templates Degree of consistent usage
Use of consistent terminology	Degree of availability of terminology: ▷ Definitions ▷ Translations Degree of consistent usage
Informed	Degree of knowing what one needs to know Degree of missing information: ▷ Knowledge domain ▷ Processes ▷ Tasks Degree of confidence in the system
Decisions	Degree of available information Degree of missing information Degree of sufficient experience
Risk management	Number of known risk profiles Degree of unknown risk profiles Degree of availability to review early warnings

External interactions

Evaluate and score your performance using the following indicators:

Element	Indicators
Communication	Degree of communication objectives Degree of addressing target audience Degree of ability to find an answer independently (self-service)
Image	Degree of customer satisfaction Degree of customer retention Degree of matching between perceived image and intended image
Service level	Number of contacts Number of complaints Average time of first response Average time of closure Degree of satisfaction of external contact Number of first-contact resolution Consistency degree on answers
Compliance	Number of known regulations Number of regulations not applied Degree of compliance with known regulations

PERSONAL EXPERIENCES AND REFLECTIONS

Evaluate your current Knowledge Management status by scoring each of following elements (0: lacking completely – 5: fully implemented/available):

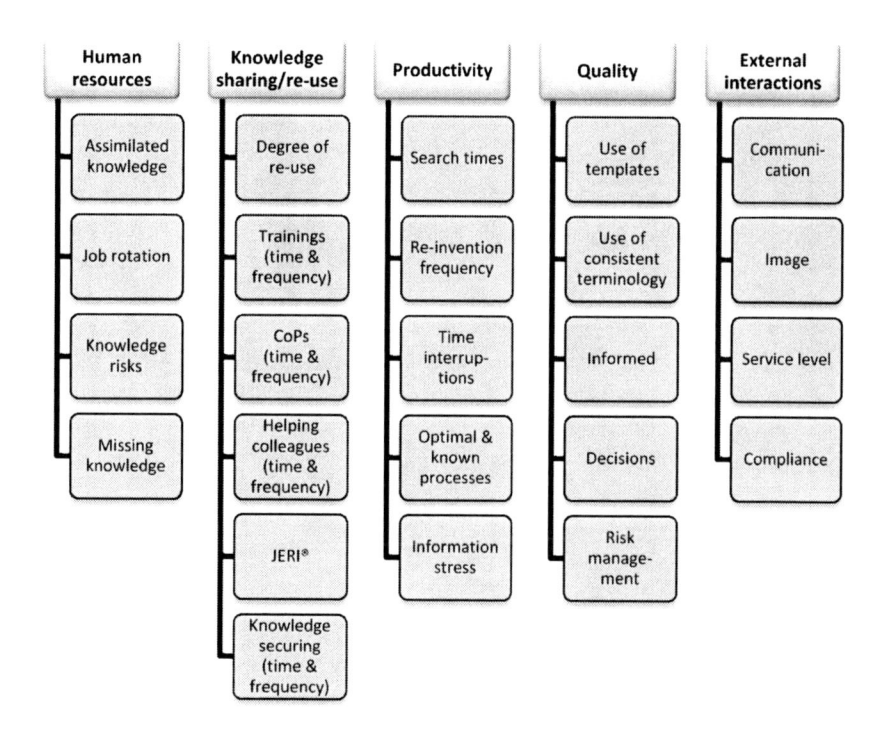

Human resources	Knowledge sharing/re-use	Productivity	Quality	External interactions
Assimilated knowledge	Degree of re-use	Search times	Use of templates	Communication
Job rotation	Trainings (time & frequency)	Re-invention frequency	Use of consistent terminology	Image
Knowledge risks	CoPs (time & frequency)	Time interruptions	Informed	Service level
Missing knowledge	Helping colleagues (time & frequency)	Optimal & known processes	Decisions	Compliance
	JERI®	Information stress	Risk management	
	Knowledge securing (time & frequency)			

Have a look on www.knowliah.eu/kcm/12 for other questions, ideas, discussion and answers on this topic.

The value of Knowledge Management

VALUE ELEMENTS

Literature provides you with long lists of possible returns of Knowledge Management. Summarised you can group them in three categories:

Quantifiable	Soft or indirect	Strategic
• Labour savings • Reinvestment of resources • Cost reduction • Cost avoidance	• Knowledge re-use • Leveraged knowledge resources • Reduced time to results/market • Customer satisfaction	• Better decisions • Improved quality • Higher customer satisfaction • Increased business and image

There are clear and less clear links between these value elements; one will not exist without another. The scheme from Skyrme Associates is a very good representation of the link between the different impacts of Knowledge Management.

RESULT DOMAINS (SKYRME ASSOCIATES)

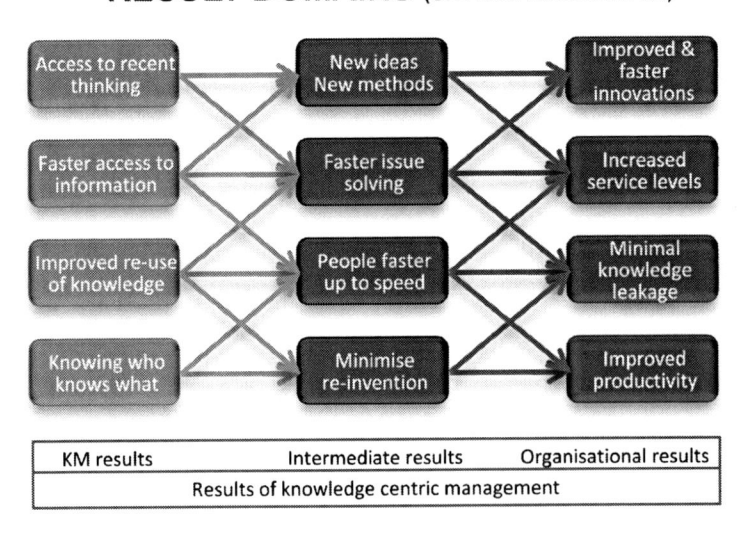

KM results	Intermediate results	Organisational results
Access to recent thinking	New ideas / New methods	Improved & faster innovations
Faster access to information	Faster issue solving	Increased service levels
Improved re-use of knowledge	People faster up to speed	Minimal knowledge leakage
Knowing who knows what	Minimise re-invention	Improved productivity

Results of knowledge centric management

FOR THE KNOWLEDGE WORKER

Most collaborators in an organisation are not interested in the organisational benefits of Knowledge Management. Only their personal hemisphere counts.

Less time to achieve the same

Too much work, too many tasks lead to pressure and stress. Each initiative reducing or easing work will have a positive reception by the individual knowledge worker.

JERI®

Too much information, too many emails, too many articles... causing more stress. Volumes of information are too big to manage everything. Initiatives delivering JERI® (Just Enough Relevant Information, when and where needed) is probably the most important potential achievement of Knowledge Management.

Better informed and knowledge aware

Personal development is another personal incentive of Knowledge Management for individuals. Intellectual challenges, knowing, be smarter are still motivators for knowledge workers.

Respected expert

In general, one is proud on being recognised, on being respected. Hierarchy is one way, expert image is a more certain way – with many more opportunities or domains – to become truly respected within, and even outside, an organisation.

FOR THE KNOWLEDGE ORGANISATION

Depending on the responsibility of a manager, or as a board member, he/she will be interested in other values of Knowledge Management.

How can revenue increase?
- ▷ Better and faster service to customers
- ▷ Better decisions based on validated information and knowledge
- ▷ Higher quality and innovation
- ▷ Smarter, better knowledge of market and competition
- ▷ Better and faster execution of business processes

Which burdens are solved?
- ▷ Too much information
- ▷ Not enough knowledge
- ▷ Loss of knowledge with reorganisation, retirement, or people leaving the organisation
- ▷ Email chaos and compliance
- ▷ Paper burden
- ▷ Disaster recovery priorities

Which financial costs can be reduced?
- ▷ Less time to find the correct information version
- ▷ Less time to find the appropriate expert
- ▷ Reduced risks
- ▷ Avoiding re-inventing the wheel

Which is the strategic value?
- ▷ Compliance with regulations and contracts
- ▷ Knowledge on strategic knowledge and information domains
- ▷ Knowledge securing and transfer
- ▷ Identification of missing knowledge
- ▷ Identification of knowledge risks

Measuring value of Knowledge Management

Actual costs

Basic approach

Only productivity-related activities can be measured. Indirect or strategic cost of not applying Knowledge Management is much harder to calculate and needs to be estimated.

Based on international studies (see also part I 'What international studies say'), and starting from a yearly average employee cost of €52,500, we can calculate the cost of the following activities for 100 collaborators.

Productivity domain	Range of costs
Search & Find	1.2 to 2.8 M€/y
Email handling	1.3 M€/y
Contract & Document management	>0.6 M€/y
Re-inventing the wheel	0.53 to 1.62 M€/y

As a very conservative and safe estimate – based on experiences with previous cases – you can take as a simple guideline:

- ▷ Indirect cost equals:
    - ▷ one (for manufacturing environments)
    - ▷ to two (for services-oriented business)
    - ▷ times the productivity costs
- ▷ The same for your Strategic cost

NOT applying Knowledge Management in an organisation of 100 collaborators has a cost of:

- ▷ 3.63 M€/y (taking minimal productivity impact)
- ▷ to 10.89 M€/y (adding indirect and strategic impact, see above)

Of course, you can argue your organisation is a very well-performing one with hard working collaborators, being twice as good as others. Bringing it down to:

- ▷ 1.8 M€/y to 5.4 M€/y

More elaborated approach

The more elaborated way of measuring your actual cost – and later on your gains – is based on the '24 elements of your Knowledge Management' status as presented earlier.

Probability of savings

Knowledge Management cannot claim to reduce these costs completely.

Your organisational context defines the potential savings. This context can be defined and used as a probability percentage based on scoring of elements like:

Is the Knowledge Management design and implementation intended to be IT supported?
Is there sufficient executive sponsorship?
Is there a genuine commitment to develop and engage managerial processes that are consistent with the goals of the Knowledge Management project?
Is your organisation open to define innovative and new processes to support the execution of the information strategy?
Have the objectives for implementing Knowledge Management been clearly articulated?
Is the contribution to the execution of the strategy understood by the employees?
Does the company have a formalised information strategy?
Is the strategy communicated throughout the organisation?
What is the quality of information?
Do you have the intention to install or maintain a formalised review policy?
Is the remuneration performance-driven (achieving goals)?
Have you developed the necessary information/communication for your employees to create buy-in?
Have all relevant implementation phases been scheduled?
What is the ambition level of Knowledge Management application?

How strong is the emphasis on re-use of knowledge in your strategy?

How strong is the emphasis on re-use of knowledge in your communications?

Do you have the intention to implement a performance-driven remuneration?

Are you planning to cascade multiple phased implementations?

Is a terminology glossary available or scheduled to be produced?

Scorings (1 to 5) combined with a weight factor per question will mostly result in probability percentages of 60% to 80%.

Again, as a very conservative and safe estimate for your organisation, you can take 50% or even lower.

Quantification of Knowledge Management value

As your Knowledge Management initiatives grow, the value of Knowledge Management will also grow for your organisation. This means that each year you should re-evaluate your progress and related value.

Implementation and investments

'No gain without pain'. Each gain will require internal and external investments. As a rule of thumb, count – in worst case – 50% to 100% of your Year 1 productivity gains as total investment.

One-third of this amount will go to external systems and coaching, and two-thirds to internal investments (mainly content creation and change of behaviour).

Second and following years: count 33% of your productivity gain as continuous internal content creation investment.

Returns

On productivity gains – based on conservative personal experiences – Knowledge Management initiatives can easily realise the following improvements (on average):

Productivity domain	Improvements
Search & Find (information and experts)	80%
Email handling and routing	35%
Contract & Document management	60%
Re-inventing the wheel	70%

Combined with earlier figures and a probability percentage of the savings of 50% returns for an organisation of 100 collaborators:

Productivity domain	Improvements
Search & Find	0,48 M€/y
Email handling	0,23 M€/y
Contract & Document management	0,18 M€/y
Re-inventing the wheel	0,18 M€/y
	1,16 M€/y

Again, to be on the safe and conservative side, we neglect any value for Indirect and Strategic returns for Year 1, and only count 50% of it for Year 2.

Total value

Combining above figures for an organisation of 100 collaborators (in million Euros per year):

Year	Investment	Productivity	Indirect Strategic	Result
1	- 1,16	1,16	0	0
2	- 0,39	1,16	0,58	1,35
3	- 0,39	1,16	1,16	1,93
4-n	- 0,39	1,16	2,32	3,09

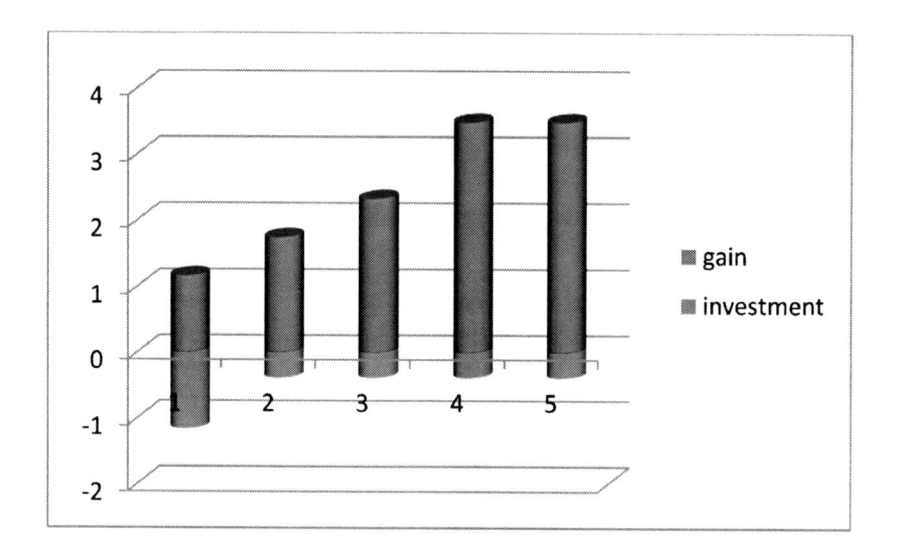

Personal experiences and reflections

Indicate your organisational probability of savings by scoring each of the following elements:

(0: lacking completely – 5: fully available)

Is the Knowledge Management design and implementation intended to be IT supported? ⬡

Is there sufficient executive sponsorship? ⬡

Is there a genuine commitment to develop and engage managerial processes that are consistent with the goals of the Knowledge Management project? ⬡

Is your organisation open to defining innovative and new processes to support the execution of the information strategy? ⬡

Have the objectives for implementing Knowledge Management been clearly articulated? ⬡

Is the contribution to the execution of the strategy understood by the employees? ⬡

Does the company have a formalised information strategy? ⬡

Is the strategy communicated throughout the organisation? ⬡

What is the quality of information? ⬡

Do you have the intention to install or maintain a formalised review policy? ⬡

Is the remuneration performance-driven (achieving goals)? ⬡

Have you developed the necessary information/communication for your employees to create buy in? ⬡

Have all relevant implementation phases been scheduled? ⬡

What is the ambition level of Knowledge Management application?

How strong is the emphasis on re-use of knowledge in your strategy?

How strong is the emphasis on re-use of knowledge in your communications?

Do you have the intention to implement a performance-driven remuneration?

Are you planning to cascade multiple phased implementations?

Is a terminology glossary available or scheduled to be produced?

Have a look on www.knowliah.eu/kcm/13 for other questions, ideas, discussion and answers on this topic.

Knowledge Management from a macro-economic perspective

EXTERNAL KNOWLEDGE MANAGEMENT

In the last decade, with the growing importance of the World Wide Web, frontiers of organisations almost vaporise with regard to available information. At the same time, all domains – technology- or service-driven – face higher complexities, more rules to comply with, etc.

Only large corporations and governments have the means to have all their required information and knowledge available internally. All other types of organisations need external experts, knowledge transfer of suppliers, and close collaboration with researchers at universities and other players in the market.

So, one of the important future challenges of Knowledge Management for each organisation is the integration of knowledge and expertise of your 'external' stakeholders/relations of your organisation.

This means:

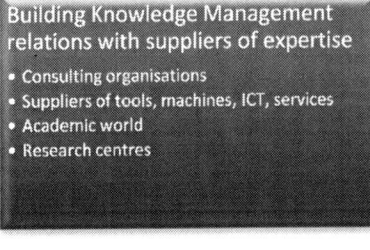

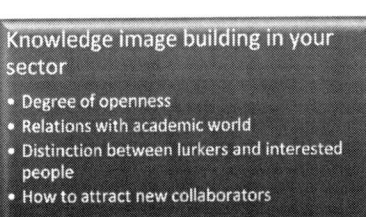

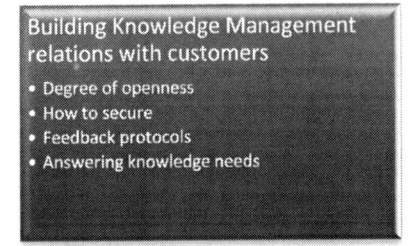

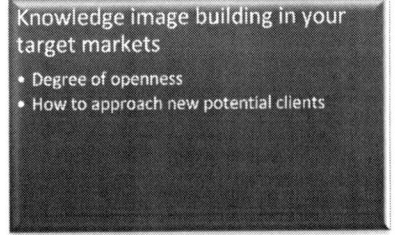

Building Knowledge Management relations with suppliers of expertise
- Consulting organisations
- Suppliers of tools, machines, ICT, services
- Academic world
- Research centres

Building Knowledge Management relations with customers
- Degree of openness
- How to secure
- Feedback protocols
- Answering knowledge needs

Knowledge image building in your sector
- Degree of openness
- Relations with academic world
- Distinction between lurkers and interested people
- How to attract new collaborators

Knowledge image building in your target markets
- Degree of openness
- How to approach new potential clients

Today, internal Knowledge Management is a competitive advantage. Tomorrow, external Knowledge Management will be your competitive advantage.

But you can only start with external Knowledge Management if your internal Knowledge Management is well organised.

FROM A GOVERNMENT PERSPECTIVE

Commercial organisations suffer more and more from competition from BRICS countries. Although Western European organisations have a high degree of productivity, they are not able to use the concentration of knowledge in and around the organisation.

Combining available knowledge and innovation will boost the knowledge economy.

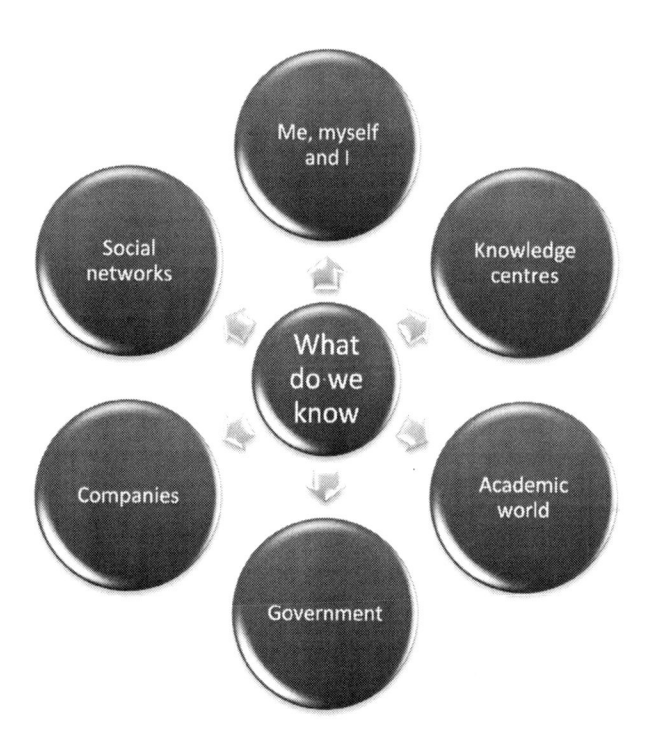

Governments can assist all types of organisations by putting emphasis on and providing means to interconnect available knowledge in regions or countries.

For all participants, this interconnection leads to:

▷ Integration of available knowledge from your neighbours, avoiding re-inventing the wheel between organisations
▷ Faster and more innovation
▷ Shorter time-to-market
▷ Minimising errors and risks
▷ A new type of business and extra revenue

For governments, this will result directly in more tax incomes and help them to be more efficient.

Nevertheless, governments still fail to understand or initiate initiatives in this domain.

From a sector perspective
Missed opportunity?

With a smaller dimension, the same is applicable for sector federations. They already perform knowledge exchange via conferences, trainings and other events.

More and more federations use and apply social networks, communities and discussion forums to interact with members.

However, they fail to capture and re-use knowledge in a structured way. Nor do they manage to make experts sufficiently visible.

Initiated by ICMS in Belgium, in collaboration with non-profit organisations V-ICT-OR and VVSG, KPLO is an exception. KPLO is a Knowledge Platform for LOcal governments, based on TiNK®4U (see part IV), interconnecting:

- ▷ Experts (automatically identified)
- ▷ Validated secured knowledge
- ▷ Non-validated information
- ▷ Questions and issues

A central knowledge role

The role of a macro-knowledge organisation can be divided into a number of tasks:

- ▷ Collecting its own articles, documents, studies, etc. and making them accessible – in other words, recording crucial knowledge (e.g. in topic groups) AND identifying relevant sources
  (supply function)
- ▷ Being a point of contact in case of questions and problems arising with regard to the sector's specialisation
  (demand function)
- ▷ Validating information and information sources with regard to correctness, usability and completeness
  (reliability function)

▷ Channelling and matching supply and demand with regard to questions and expertise available in the network
(connection function)

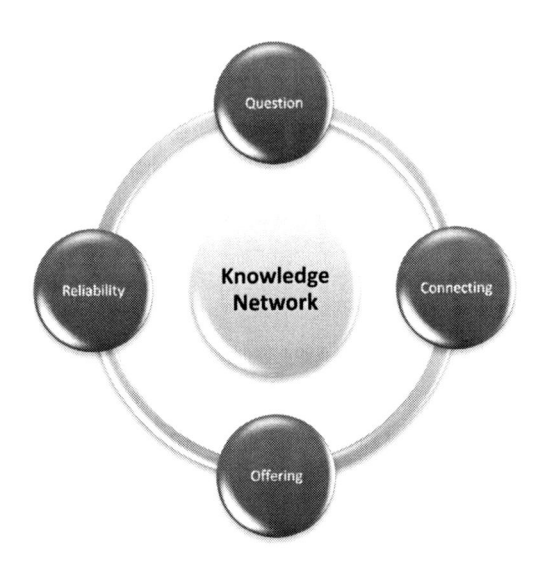

Diagram: Knowledge Network with four surrounding nodes — Question, Connecting, Offering, Reliability.

A knowledge-network organisation can – even with current staffing levels – get more out of the available potential of its members and topic groups.

Personal experiences and reflections

List relevant information and knowledge sources for your organisation:

- ▷ Sector and trade organisations
- ▷ Suppliers
- ▷ Academic world
- ▷ Government
- ▷ Competition
- ▷ Others

Have a look on www.knowliah.eu/kcm/14 for other questions, ideas, discussion and answers on this topic.

PART IV

A NEW APPROACH: KNOWLEDGE MANAGEMENT MADE EASY AND QUICK

This section is about a new innovative approach to Knowledge Management, making a Knowledge Management initiative easier to start, with much faster direct returns for the organisation.

So, forget the traditional unsuccessful approaches of securing and sharing, and communities.

A new approach

Classic Knowledge Management approaches

Securing and sharing

The typical Knowledge Management approach is based on a *knowledge development approach*.

In this approach, knowledge development is managed and people are identified and instructed to develop and capture knowledge in their area of expertise.

This requires extra time and effort, where one is never sure if the secured knowledge will be used at all.

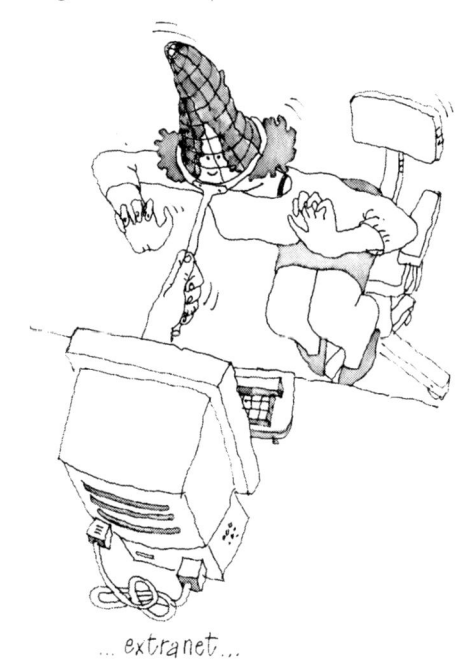

... extranet ...

Generally, this approach already fails after one to two months, mainly for the following reasons:

> ▷ It means a threat for the expert: he/she is forced to 'share' his/her knowledge, making the organisation less dependent
>
> ▷ It means extra work for the expert, where after some weeks other priorities always come first
>
> ▷ For the end-user the pile of *too much information* is just growing, making the information stress greater

Communities of Practice

Another applied approach is setting up *Communities of Practices* or *Communities of Interests*.

It is an electronic platform where you allow people to discuss in an electronic format and to share information.

When you want to learn more on CoPs, you should read the book *Communities of practice: learning, meaning, and identity* by *Etienne Wenger* from 1999.

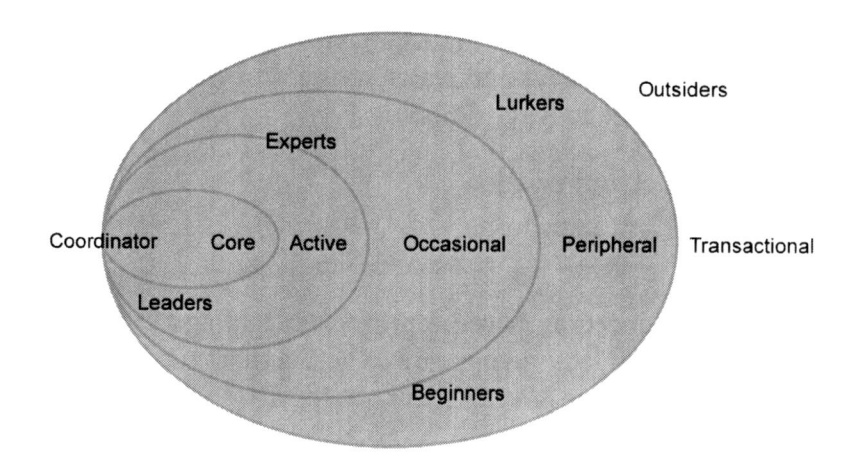

The positive element on CoPs is the effectiveness on the demolition of hierarchical borders in Taylorian organisations. It allows people to interact with each other and to cultivate a culture of collaboration and working as a team.

The weak points of this approach can be summarised as:

▷ Being alive as a community largely depends on the coordinator and five to seven core people actively contributing to the community
▷ CoPs almost always lack mechanisms and procedures to capture produced knowledge in a re-usable format
▷ When you are not part of the discussion you will not know or be aware that such information/knowledge exists

QUESTION-DRIVEN APPROACH

Addressing the issues of knowledge workers is the starting point for organisational Knowledge Management.

Knowledge Management initiatives often fail because of their emphasis on the knowledge organisation. Knowledge, however, starts with and depends on your knowledge workers. You can start with huge change management initiatives to achieve your Knowledge Management objectives as an organisation. The best motivator for change is the support a person gets that facilitates his work.

To achieve your Knowledge Management objectives, we at ICMS Group believe it is easier and faster to maximise the support of knowledge workers in three domains:

▷ Too much information
▷ Insufficient knowledge
▷ Lost knowledge

Starting with a question-driven approach and adding a knowledge-building approach later on appears to be the most successful and pragmatic Knowledge Management strategy.

AND, as *a result* of supporting your knowledge workers, you will achieve your organisational Knowledge Management objectives much more easily, faster and with more enthusiasm from your co-workers.

It allows organisations to start with a *question-driven approach*, benefit immediately and grow as needed by adding a *knowledge development approach*.

Without a question to be answered
or an issue to be solved
there is no direct reason
to invest time and money
in securing knowledge

WHAT IS A QUESTION-DRIVEN SOLUTION?

A knowledge platform

TiNK®4U is:

▷ A unified information/knowledge access engine, aimed at finding answers

▷ Also a knowledge development and knowledge securing platform where questions, available information and experts are linked smoothly to each other

▷ And results in knowledge re-use, bringing real value to your knowledge

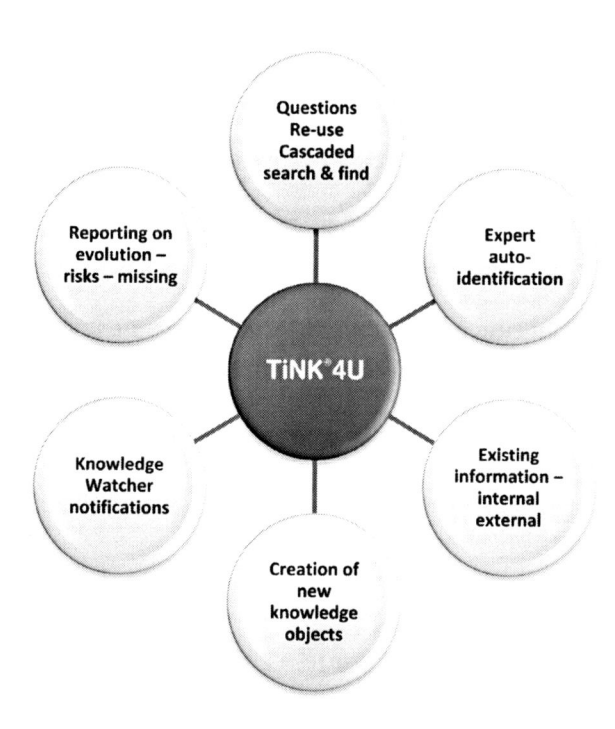

TiNK®4U

- Questions Re-use Cascaded search & find
- Expert auto-identification
- Existing information – internal external
- Creation of new knowledge objects
- Knowledge Watcher notifications
- Reporting on evolution – risks – missing

It allows organisations to start with a *question-driven approach*, benefit immediately and grow as needed by adding a *knowledge development approach*.

Knowledge and Information Management becomes part of the day-to-day work of the knowledge worker. TiNK°4U aims to:

▷ Deliver a high performance workplace for the knowledge worker

▷ Help an organisation manage and continue to create its biggest asset – knowledge

TiNK°4U (base) delivers a cascaded search & find with integrated development and capturing of knowledge. TiNK°4U (extension) also delivers knowledge-reporting features for better management and steering.

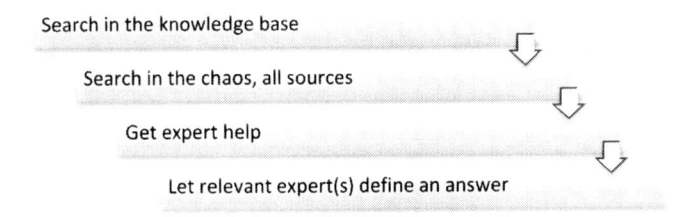

Search in the knowledge base ⇩

Search in the chaos, all sources ⇩

Get expert help ⇩

Let relevant expert(s) define an answer

Incorporating reliability

Not all information and knowledge has the same level of reliability or is maintained with the same level of care.

The highest reliability ($R1$) is achieved when you are sure that:

▷ A known person with relevant expertise has written something down

▷ This person has enriched it with context (domain, target audience etc.)

▷ It was validated by another person with relevant expertise

▷ The information/knowledge is maintained (freshness date)

At a level below that ($R2$) is information that originates from known relevant external sources but does not come with the guarantee that the four above-mentioned parameters are present. Usually, only two or three requirements have been met.

At a level below that (*R3*) is information that originates from known relevant external sources, but only meets one or two of the requirements.

In a knowledge environment such as TiNK°4U, these different levels of reliability are fully taken into account.

Essential features

The essential features of this knowledge platform driven by demand and supply include:

- ▷ All your different information sources become accessible
- ▷ Employees no longer search, but FIND instead and can start browsing thanks to:
    - ▷ automatic grouping per subject
    - ▷ 'one-click text mining' features
- ▷ Employees are better informed and no longer drown in the abundance of information (JERI® – Just Enough Relevant Information, when and where needed)
- ▷ Automatic integration of knowledge development and capturing
- ▷ A clear distinction between validated, maintained and enriched information (knowledge) and the collection of all non-validated sources
- ▷ Simple identification of the right expert(s) inside or outside the organisation
- ▷ A structured and unstructured approach in combination with a minimum of effort, both at start-up as well as in operation

TiNK®4U helps you to control your knowledge sharing and knowledge capturing and make the chaos accessible, without additional effort.

Personal experiences and reflections

List the last five encountered problems and issues in your own job.

Ask 10 other colleagues to list their last five encountered problems and issues in their functions.

Group those encountered problems and issues in domains.

Identify the approach followed to answer the question or solve the issue:

▷ Own investigation in the organisation
▷ Search the Web
▷ Take the phone
▷ Mail to all potential respondents
▷ Drop the question in a community

Have a look on www.knowliah.eu/kcm/15 for other questions, ideas, discussion and answers on this topic.

Implementing Knowledge Management easily with quick wins

Overview

Implementation is scoped and linked to your specific needs and phasing. In a start-up meeting, objectives, scope and planning are agreed upon and your internal efforts and your supplier's effort and tasks (or those of its consulting partner's) are defined.

Implementation is focused on assistance in the different elements of the Knowledge Management implementation process. As such, we identify the following structure:

Build knowledge on Knowledge Management ▷ Static preparation phase ▷ Dynamic operational phase ▷ Extension phase

▷ Build knowledge on Knowledge Management
   ▷ Workshop on business perspective
   ▷ Workshop on implementing Knowledge Management
▷ Static preparation phase
   ▷ Phase 1: accessibility (to all available information, validated and non-validated)
   ▷ Phase 2: experts (identification based on contribution)
   ▷ Phase 3: securing (capturing requested knowledge into validated information)
▷ Dynamic operational phase
   ▷ Phase 4: operational usage
   ▷ Phase 5: proactive knowledge building (capturing of strategic future-oriented domains)
▷ Extension phase
   ▷ Phase 6: knowledge reporting (usage, risk, evolution)
   ▷ Phase 7: limited accessibility for customers and suppliers (self-service and building knowledge image)

Preparation phase
Accessibility

An operationally usable and unified information access tool (search & find engine) that can be used immediately and that provides:

- ▷ Consolidated access to all information sources
- ▷ Automatic subject grouping
- ▷ Text-mining effects
- ▷ Find for similar information
- ▷ Respect for current security rules.

Activity

1. Identify all potential information sources (file servers, ERP, document management systems, portals, databases, etc.) and indicate their level of reliability
2. Analyse integration capabilities and security
3. Install
4. Configure collections and connections
5. Configure synonyms and translations
6. Set up integration with 'special' sources
7. Set up security
8. Initial indexing

Experts

When a search result is insufficient or too complex to understand, the integrated Expert Locator helps users to identify the currently most relevant expert(s) to:

▷ Explain the answers
▷ Provide them with additional better answers

	Activity
1	Manual or automated feed of relevant documents to calculate one's expert profile
2	Develop potential mechanism to identify one's expertise automatically (e.g. private folders, email replies, project files, document management system)
3	Automate mechanism to identify one's expertise
4	Determine degree of integration of knowledge base content in the author profile
5	If based on manual provision of relevant documents by the expert, an internal procedure is required

Securing

Completion of the preparation for the use of TiNK®4U.

As a result of this phase, you will have defined the rules related to:

- ▷ Validated knowledge is stored in a knowledge base
  - ▷ to share
  - ▷ to maintain
- ▷ The use of the system, to limit interruptions for the experts
- ▷ The answering of questions in a knowledge object (wording, style, granularity)
- ▷ Collaboration and production of content in a forum
- ▷ Validation of content by other relevant experts

Activity

1. Configure the knowledge base.

   Modify, remove or add values of context elements like K domain, K sub-domain, K sub-sub-domain, Process, Product, Service, Target audience, Confidentiality

2. Import validated information

3. Define rules for end-users with regard to the use of TiNK®4U related to:

   - ▷ limiting interruptions for experts
   - ▷ adding content to the knowledge base

4. Define rules for experts with regard to answering questions and capturing this information in a knowledge object

5. Define rules for experts with regard to collaboration in a forum

6. Define rules for experts with regard to validation, approval and maintenance of knowledge objects

7. Define templates and structures for other information types such as:

   - ▷ specifications
   - ▷ how to procedures
   - ▷ tips and tricks

8. Integrate rules in the home page of the system

DYNAMIC OPERATIONAL PHASE

Operational usage

The starting point is an empty knowledge base to:

- ▷ Provide unified access to all information, automatically presented in subject trees, allowing for direct reuse
- ▷ Allow for the adding of relevant information and answers as validated/tested information
- ▷ Build a knowledge base that answers a real and current need
- ▷ Be informed of personal relevant information

	Activity
1	Communicate instructions with regard to usage
2	Communicate instructions with regard to answering and creating knowledge objects
3	Communicate instructions with regard to forum collaboration
4	Monitor daily usage

Proactive knowledge building

As a result of this phase, an organisation will:

- ▷ Identify relevant experts per domain and sub-domain
- ▷ Build and extend its knowledge base with extra strategic knowledge topics:
  - ▷ what should other departments know on your activities?
  - ▷ what is the minimum your people in the department should know?

In turn, this will lead to:

▷ Better informed people
▷ Better use and re-use of available validated information
▷ Conversion to a knowledge-centred organisation

	Activity
1	Identify important knowledge domains
2	Identify strategic domains with relevant responsible experts
3	Start build and capture knowledge

Extension phase

Knowledge reporting

Evaluate usage and importance

Do not secure and maintain knowledge just for the sake of it. Around 80% of the information in an organisation is hardly used. Why should you put time and energy into securing knowledge in validated information if the specific domain is never used?

Next to usage, you also need to re-evaluate the strategic importance of all your domains; the world is changing quite fast.

Results

As a result of this phase, an organisation will receive the following reports (based on semantic network analysis):

- An inventory of important knowledge topics with their inter-relations
- A report monitoring the evolution of knowledge topics:
  - new topics appearing
  - existing topics disappearing
- A report with the knowledge risks:
  - white spots (missing knowledge compared to strategic goals)
  - black holes (domains weakly supported by experts)

Activity
1. Install TiNK°4U – extensions
2. Configure the environment
3. Carry out roll-out of TiNK°4U extensions
4. Use TiNK°4U extensions

Limited accessibility for stakeholders (self-service)

As a result of this phase, an organisation will be able to expose its valuable knowledge in a secured way to its external professional relations:

▷ Customers having access to personal relevant knowledge
▷ Optimised communication means with all stakeholders of the organisation
▷ Know the external needs on your information and knowledge

Activity

1 Install separate external TiNK®4U
2 Configure the environment
3 Carry out roll-out of external TiNK®4U extensions
4 Use externalTiNK®4U extensions

PERSONAL EXPERIENCES AND REFLECTIONS

Consolidate and list the 20 most important information sources for your organisation.

Indicate per source the reliability (0 to 10: most important).

Identify the most relevant source (or combination) to automatically calculate expert profiles:

- ▷ Sent mails
- ▷ Personal folder
- ▷ Owned knowledge objects
- ▷ Written documents
- ▷ Answered questions
- ▷ Etc.

Have a look on www.knowliah.eu/kcm/16 *for other questions, ideas, discussion and answers on this topic.*

Results and reports

Results

In each phase

The use of Knowledge Management with this approach results in *clear benefits.*

Individual	Intermediate	Organisation
• Faster find • JERI®, being better informed • Access to the most relevant expert	• Faster problem-solving • Reduced risks • Better decisions • More effective hires • Minimisation of re-invention	• Productivity/performance • Improved customer service • Market intelligence • Better/faster innovation • Reducing knowledge loss/leakage

Generally, TiNK® results in a productivity increase of 30% to 70% with regard to information, communication and knowledge activities or 1.5% to 15% with regard to total efficiency of the organisation.

This is visible in:

▷ **Labour savings** thanks to re-use of information
▷ **Re-allocation of resources** to other important business processes
▷ **Cost reduction** thanks to less people and less time required
▷ **Cost avoidance** since actual resources will have more capacity

Even when you opt for a phased implementation, spread in time, each phase results directly in clear benefits:

Phase	Topic	Most important benefit and result
1	Accessibility	Consolidated finding in all your sources with automated subject-grouping, text-mining, duplicate and near-duplicate detection
2	Experts	Find the most relevant expert based on fully-automated expert-profiles Interruptions of the experts are limited Experts are acknowledged and become respected in specific knowledge domains (based on contributions)
3	Securing	Validated knowledge is stored in a knowledge base to be shared and maintained ▷ create once ▷ reuse often Build a knowledge base that answers a real and current need and be informed of personal relevant information The knowledge securing process is structured and supported
4	Operational usage	Knowledge capturing work is integrated in everyday tasks ▷ by individuals with validation of co-workers or domain responsible (approval) ▷ by groups of experts (forum)

Phase	Topic	Most important benefit and result
5	Proactive knowledge-building	Relevant experts per domain and sub-domain are identified and your organisation will build and extend its knowledge base with extra strategic knowledge topics Up-front knowledge development work can be avoided (or limited): ▷ the knowledge need drives the creation of knowledge objects (outside-in approach) ▷ up-front creation of knowledge in strategic domains is still possible (inside-out approach)
6	Knowledge reporting	An inventory of important knowledge topics with their inter-relations and evolution reports on knowledge risks: white spots (knowledge risks) and black holes (missing knowledge)
7	Limited accessibility for customers and suppliers (self-service)	Optimised communication means with all stakeholders of the organisation Know the external needs on your information and knowledge

Value of Knowledge Management

A non-satisfactory answer is 'zero' since most organisations tend to focus on Knowledge MANAGEMENT instead of Knowledge RE-USE.

The real value only appears when co-workers USE and APPLY available information, knowledge and expertise.

Asking for the returns is a valid investment question (although in most cases it also indicates the lack of belief in Knowledge Management).

As in most areas, there is no straight answer to this question. The answer depends on elements like: objective, time-line, culture, probability of savings, completion of the conditions for success, etc.

Knowledge centric Management has an impact on the operations and results of the complete organisation. Organisational VALUE areas that KcM delivers are:

- How can revenue increase?
  - better and faster services to customers
  - better decisions
  - higher quality and innovation
  - smarter, better knowledge of market and competition
  - better and faster execution of business processes
- What burdens are solved?
  - too much information
  - not enough knowledge
  - loss of knowledge
  - email chaos and compliance
  - paper burden
  - disaster recovery priorities

- What financial costs can be reduced?
  - less time to find the correct information version
  - less time to find the appropriate expert
  - reduced risks
  - avoiding re-inventing the wheel
- What is the strategic value?
  - compliance
  - knowledge on strategic knowledge and information domains
  - knowledge securing and transfer
  - identification of missing knowledge and knowledge risks

Each of the above elements has a quantifiable and non-quantifiable component, where the non-quantifiable will have a valorisation of one to five times the quantifiable ones.

You can use the above elements to estimate your returns, or you can use an appropriate selection of the '24 elements to evaluate KcM' mentioned earlier in this book (Chapter 12).

Reports

Evolution report

Based on semantic network analysis (knowledge topic network), TiNK®4U is able to report a ranking of knowledge domains and their interaction.

Repeating this reporting on a monthly basis provides organisations with a knowledge evolution report that indicates changes in ranking and inter-relation.

Knowledge risk reports

A mapping with an organisation's expert profiles gives an indication of its knowledge risks: domains that are insufficiently covered by experts (black holes). The reports list the domains that are weakly covered by experts (e.g. only covered by two experts; configurable).

White spots, missing knowledge reports

A mapping with an organisation's strategic knowledge domains (that it wishes to cover in the future) gives an indication of your actual knowledge gaps (white spots). The reports list the domains that are not actually covered by experts.

PERSONAL EXPERIENCES AND REFLECTIONS

How would you use and benefit from these reports?

- ▷ Evolution report
- ▷ Knowledge risk reports
- ▷ White spots, missing knowledge reports

What other reports would be required in this context? Any suggestions?

Have a look on www.knowliah.eu/kcm/17 for other questions, ideas, discussion and answers on this topic.

Appendices

Author

Hans Van Heghe (°1965) is the founder and managing director of ICMS Group. He has a broad background in IT and is an industrial engineer by education, with an economics/management orientation (IPO). He has gained extensive management experience at, among others, Texas Instruments, Bekaert, Lernout & Hauspie (product manager), FICS (unit manager) and write! (general manager).

Since 1999, Hans has been an MBA lecturer in Information and Knowledge Management at the United Business Institutes in Brussels. He is a frequent guest speaker on topics such as practical Knowledge Management implementations, generic information management, Knowledge Management and innovation.

As a strategic thinker/advisor, he has assisted over 200 organisations in developing a vision and roadmap towards Information and Knowledge Management – organisations ranging from SMEs to large corporations, in both the private and public sector.

Furthermore, from 2004 to 2007, he was Chairman of the non-profit organisation Project Management Belgium. This organisation offers a network platform and knowledge base for its members, making project management more accessible. From 2008 to 2010 he was a board member of the non-profit organisation Salve Strategi. This organisation offers a network platform and knowledge base for its members on more elaborated strategic thinking, both for commercial organisations and governments.

ICMS Group

The Belgian organisation ICMS Group is one of the leaders in the field of information management in Europe. ICMS Group develops intelligent solutions for Information and Knowledge Management.

ICMS Group takes a different approach, which produces a remarkably better result. Or, as one of our customers put it: "In the correlation between method — functionality — user-friendliness — price, ICMS Group is the number one by far."

Our objective is to provide clear, added-value solutions and services to our customers in their pursuit of optimal management of information and knowledge, which results in:

▷ Increased operational productivity
▷ Better internal and external communication
▷ Secured capturing of the information and knowledge in the organisation

TiNK® METHOD

As an alternative for the unstructured information and knowledge in an organisation, ICMS Group has developed the TiNK® method, which focuses on human cognition.

TiNK® is an alternative that deals with information in a flexible and dynamic way on the basis of contextual enrichment. TiNK® is short for Transferring Information aNd Knowledge.

The TiNK® method describes the processes in the human brain related to the storage and transfer of knowledge and information. The TiNK® method has been validated by research from the K.U.Leuven.

TiNK® represents a total approach for information with:

- Automatic enrichment and categorisation
- Dynamic views for multi-dimensional browsing
- Through information contextual and full-text search
- Re-use of information objects
- Dynamic associations
- Security of information
- Flexible workflows

For more details see the Ecademy Press book *Learning to swim in information*.